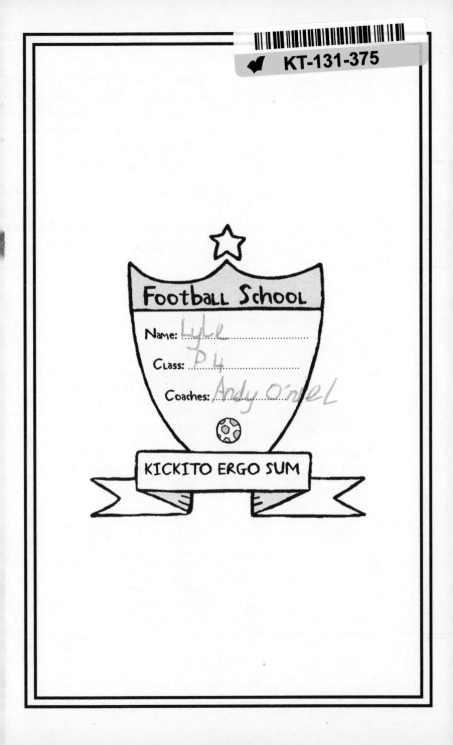

Football School

Name: Lyle

Class: P4

Coaches: Andy O'niel

KICKITO ERGO SUM

To BNZ – A.B.
To ABC – B.L.
For my dad – S.G.

First published 2018 by Walker Books Ltd
87 Vauxhall Walk, London SE11 5HJ

2 4 6 8 10 9 7 5 3 1

Text © 2018 Alex Bellos and Ben Lyttleton
Illustrations © 2018 Spike Gerrell

The right of Alex Bellos and Ben Lyttleton, and Spike Gerrell
to be identified as authors and illustrator respectively of this work has been
asserted by them in accordance with the Copyright, Designs and Patents Act 1988

This book has been typeset in Palatino

Printed and bound by CPI Group (UK) Ltd, Croydon CR0 4YY

British Library Cataloguing in Publication Data:
a catalogue record for this book is available from the British Library

ISBN 978-1-4063-7958-7

WALKER
BOOKS

FSC
www.fsc.org
MIX
Paper from
responsible sources
FSC® C020471

www.walker.co.uk
www.footballschool.co

F⚽⚽TBALL SCHOOL
THE AMAZING QUIZ BOOK

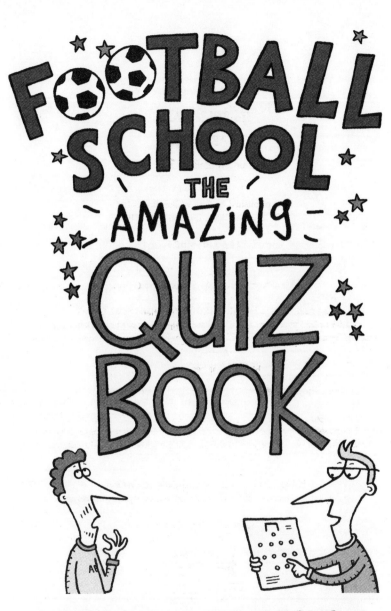

Alex Bellos & Ben Lyttleton
Illustrated by Spike Gerrell

HELLO, everyone! WELCOME to Football School's Amazing Quiz Book.

It's a World Cup football special! I'm ALEX.

And I'm Ben. We're your quizmasters!

We have written more than 300 questions that will test your knowledge about international football.

The World Cup is the most exciting tournament in football – and a great way to discover fascinating facts about the world! You'll discover:

What a white elephant is...

The dog who saved the World Cup. Woof, woof!

How to count in five different languages...

The World Cup winner named after one of Snow White's dwarves...

And whether this is the right sign for an indirect free kick...

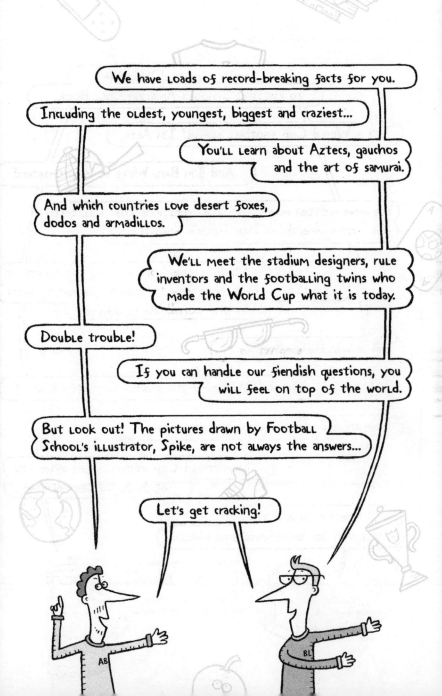

CONTENTS

Test your World Cup knowledge!

Find the answers on page 168. But no cheating!

WONDERFUL WORLD

We're going to kick off with a fact you definitely know: football is the most popular sport in the world. Over 250 million people play football, and billions watch the game on TV. The tournament we look forward to the most is the World Cup, when the best footballing nations compete against each other. It only comes around every four years, but like everything that you need patience for, it's worth the wait when it arrives. Nothing is more exciting than watching your country play in a World Cup. We love it!

The World Cup has been held every four years since 1930, almost a century ago, with only one small break break between 1938 and 1950. The Women's World Cup has been held every four years since 1991. That's a lot of matches, stadiums, goals and heroes to talk about – and we're going to be learning all about the glory and heartbreak in this book. But to begin with, we're going on a global tour around all the countries that have hosted this amazing event. Got your passports? All aboard!

1. **Uruguay hosted and won the first ever World Cup in 1930. It is also the country that has the most *what* per person in the world?**

   a) Toilet paper
   b) Copies of *Football School*
   c) Manchester United replica shirts
   d) Cows ✓

2. **Every match in the 1930 World Cup took place in Uruguay's capital city. What is its name?**

   a) Montevideo ✓
   b) Montephone
   c) Monteradio
   d) Monteyoutube

3. **Italy hosted the second World Cup in 1934. FIFA promised that it would switch continents for the next one, but changed its mind and the third World Cup took place in 1938 in another European country, France. Which two teams were so upset they refused to play?**

   a) France and Italy
   b) Italy and Brazil
   c) England and Argentina
   d) Argentina and Uruguay ✓

4. **The World Cup has been held every four years since 1930 except for a gap between 1938 and 1950. This was because:**

   a) It rained non-stop for 12 years.

   b) Many countries were fighting in the Second World War from 1939 to 1945. ✓

   c) Everyone was too busy playing cricket.

   d) FIFA lost the trophy and were really embarrassed.

5. **Brazil hosted the World Cup for the first time in 1950. In what two ways did Brazilian soldiers salute the Brazil team when they came out to play their opening match?**

   a) They shot blanks from 21 guns and released 5,000 pigeons into the air. ✓

   b) They launched a giant inflatable banana and performed a street dance to the national anthem.

   c) They drove a tank painted yellow onto the centre of the pitch, and fired a man dressed as a toucan out the top.

   d) They spread out a flag across the pitch, and released onto it a selection of local wildlife including armadillos, anteaters, tapirs, sloths, macaques, caimans, spiders and beetles.

6. These countries are all World Cup hosts.
   Find each country on the map.

YEAR	HOST
1930	Uruguay 6
1934	Italy 13
1938	France 10
1950	Brazil 3
1954	Switzerland 11
1958	Sweden 7
1962	Chile 4
1966	England 8
1970	Mexico 2
1974	West Germany 9
1978	Argentina 5
1982	Spain 12
1986	Mexico 2
1990	Italy 13
1994	USA 1
1998	France 10
2002	Japan/ South Korea 16
2006	Germany 9
2010	South Africa 18
2014	Brazil 3
2018	Russia 14
2022	Qatar 17

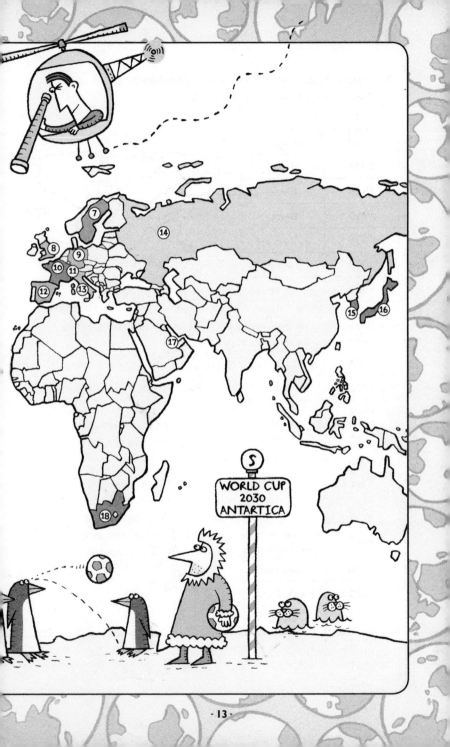

7. **England beat West Germany 4–2 in the 1966 World Cup final, played on home soil at Wembley Stadium. What did England substitute Ian Callaghan keep in his pocket during the game?**

   a) A German sausage that
      he stroked for good luck
   b) The hairbrush of captain Bobby Moore
   c) Coach Alf Ramsey's pre-match team talk
   d) The false teeth of teammate Nobby Stiles ✓

8. **Victory against West Germany in the 1966 final is the only time England have won the trophy. The match is also special because of which of the following facts, which still holds true to this day?**

   a) The highest attendance at a World Cup final
   b) The most watched football match in English TV history, with 32 million viewers tuning in ✓
   c) The only time World Cup winners have worn white shorts
   d) The only time West Germany have lost a World Cup final

9. **The 1974 World Cup was held in West Germany. It was also the only time that two German teams took part, as the country at that time was split in two for political reasons. West Germany won the tournament but they lost in the group stages to the other German team. What was it called?**

   a) North Germany
   b) Prussia
   c) South Germany
   d) East Germany ✓

10. **Colombia won the right to host the 1986 World Cup but withdrew four years before the tournament began. What reason did president Belisario Betancur give for the decision?**

a) He preferred baseball to football.
b) The country did not have enough money to host the event. ✓
c) He was worried Colombia might lose every match.
d) He did not like Colombia's kit.

11. **Which Asian country was the first to host a World Cup, staging the women's competition in 1991?**

a) Japan
b) India
c) China ✓
d) Vietnam

12. **What FIFA competition is played exactly a year before the World Cup? Since 2005 it has been held in the nation that will host the World Cup as a trial run for the bigger tournament.**

a) Rehearsal Cup
b) One-More-Year Cup
c) Cuppy Cup
d) Confederations Cup ✓

13. **Which World Cup host country produced the tournament's biggest average crowds of over 65,000 per match?**

a) Brazil (1950)
b) USA (1994) ✓
c) Germany (2006)
d) Brazil (2014)

14. **The Italian capital city Rome hosted the 1990 World Cup final. The biggest sports venue of ancient Rome was called the Circus Maximus, which had a capacity of approximately 250,000 people. What sport took place there?**

a) Football
b) Clown racing
c) Rhythmic gymnastics
d) Chariot racing ✓

15. USA became the first host country to win the Women's World Cup on home soil in 1999. What was the team's nickname?

a) The Totally Awesomes
b) The 99ers
c) The Ballers
d) The Mad Hatters

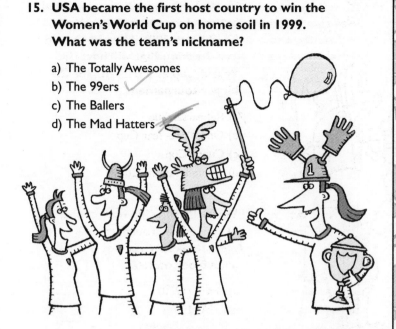

16. Why was the 2002 World Cup in Japan and South Korea unique?

a) It was the first and only time two countries have jointly hosted the tournament.
b) It was the first and only time FIFA organized a singing competition for fans.
c) It was the first and only time mascots were used as assistant referees.
d) It was the first and only time players were allowed to wear fancy dress.

17. Complete the sentence from Jürgen Klinsmann, who coached the 2006 World Cup host Germany, and went on to coach USA in the 2014 World Cup. After Germany finished third in 2006, he said:

"Everyone feels that the national team is ..."

a) "The team of the most handsome boys in the land." ✓

b) "A bunch of losers."

c) "The best in the world."

d) "Their team." ✓

18. What is unusual about the World Cup 2018 host city Kaliningrad?

a) It's the first World Cup city to have 11 letters in its name.

b) It is in an area of Russia sandwiched between Poland and Lithuania, which is not connected to the Russian mainland. ✓

c) Its footballers wear linen jerseys.

d) The city's emblem is a football.

19. Which country does not border France, host of the 2019 Women's World Cup?

a) Belgium

b) Italy

c) Germany

d) Netherlands ✓

20. Match the famous landmark to the city that has hosted a World Cup final.

a) Rio, Brazil ✓   b) Munich, Germany
c) Yokohama, Japan   d) Paris, France
e) California, USA   f) London, UK

1)

2)

3)

4)

5)

6)

GREAT GOALS

What is football without goals? They are the moments we remember, the efforts we celebrate, and, of course, they are the difference between winning and losing.

To score a goal in a World Cup has to be the high point of any player's career. And to score the winning goal in the final of a World Cup is probably the single most thrilling experience in all of football. In this chapter we want to celebrate the World Cup's goal-scoring legends and relive some of their most famous goals.

These goals are sometimes the result of individual brilliance and sometimes the result of amazing teamwork. A great goal is like a work of art, it's beautiful and spellbinding to behold.

When a World Cup goal is scored, entire countries celebrate. If you are watching your national team in a World Cup and they score a goal, you can hear the cheers all down the street. Open the scoring!

1. **The player who scores the most goals in the World Cup wins an award called the Golden Boot. Between 1982 and 2010 this award was called:**

a) The Golden Goal

b) The Golden Foot

c) The Golden Shoe ✓

d) The Golden Toe

2. **What move is Brazil centre-forward Leônidas da Silva – who top-scored in the 1938 World Cup with seven goals – credited with inventing during the quarter-final win over Czechoslovakia?**

a) Tandem kick

b) Unicycle kick

c) Bicycle kick ✓

d) Tricycle kick

3. **Brazil striker Pelé made his name on the world stage at the 1958 World Cup when he was just 17, scoring the winner against Wales in the quarter-final and a hat-trick against France in the semi-final. In the final, he scored two more to make it a 5–2 win over Sweden. His first goal in that game was a brilliant volley, but what did he do just before striking the ball?**

a) Chipped the ball over a defender's head ✓

b) Tied his shoelaces

c) Shook hands with the referee

d) Flashed his bottom at the goalkeeper

4. **Diego Maradona scored one of the greatest individual goals of all time against England in the quarter-final of the 1986 World Cup. He ran from the halfway line and dribbled past five players, including the goalkeeper, before kicking the ball into the net. What did Maradona say when teammate Jorge Valdano asked why he didn't pass to him?**

a) "I wanted to, but all these English guys were in the way, by the time they were gone I had scored!" ✓

b) "I knew I could do it on my own!"

c) "It would have been too easy!"

d) "Because you are smelly!"

5. The goal of the tournament of the 1991 Women's World Cup was scored by Swedish midfielder Ingrid Johansson in a 3-2 defeat to USA. How did she score the goal?

a) Header from the penalty spot

b) Curling shot from a corner-kick

c) Overhead-kick from edge of the area

d) Shot from 40 yards ✓

6. **What links Pelé (Brazil 1958), Geoff Hurst (England 1966), Dick Nanninga (Netherlands 1978) and Zinedine Zidane (France 1998)?**

   a) They all scored headers in a World Cup final. ✓
   b) They all scored hat-tricks in a World Cup final.
   c) They all scored own goals in a World Cup final.
   d) They top-scored in the competition without scoring in a World Cup final.

7. **Dennis Bergkamp was one of the Netherlands' best players in the 1980s and 1990s. How did he describe his goal in the 1998 World Cup quarter-final against Argentina, when he controlled a 50-yard pass with his first touch, skipped past his marker with his second and scored with his third?**

a) "I closed my eyes and hoped for the best."

b) "I might have been offside."

c) "It's like your life has led up to this moment." ✓

d) "Sorry, but I can't talk about it without crying."

8. **Germany beat Sweden 2–1 in the final of the 2003 Women's World Cup when Nia Künzer scored with a header in the eighth minute of extra time. This practice of ending a knock-out match as soon as a goal has been scored in extra time was also used in the 1998 and 2002 World Cups. By what name was it known?**

   a) Sudden Death
   b) Stoppage Stopper
   c) Golden Goal ✓
   d) Squeaky Bum Time

9. **Andrés Iniesta scored Spain's winning goal in the 2010 World Cup final. What type of sportsman did his former coach at Barcelona, Tito Vilanova, compare him to when he said, "Andrés doesn't run, he glides... Sssswishhh, sssswishhh, sssswishhh"?**

   a) Ice hockey player ✓
   b) Hang-glider
   c) Gymnast
   d) Deep-sea diver

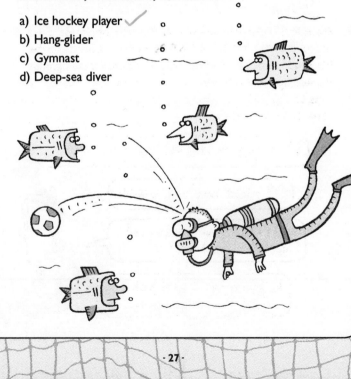

10. **What prize did USA forward Abby Wambach win for her last-minute header in the 2011 Women's World Cup quarter-final against Brazil?**

a) The Golden Boot for top goalscorer in the competition

b) An award for the greatest goal scored in the Women's World Cup following a vote on the FIFA website ✓

c) The Presidential Medal of Freedom, the highest honour for an American citizen

d) A lifetime supply of her favourite brand of trainers

11. **Ireland striker Stephanie Roche has scored in two consecutive World Cup qualifying campaigns. But what did she do for her club side Peamount United in 2013, that made her famous all over the world?**

a) She scored the first "double hat-trick" in the history of football.

b) She scored with a volley that was voted second in FIFA's goal of the year competition. ✓

c) She replaced the referee who was sick but then scored a goal for her team.

d) She scored a hat-trick of own goals.

12. **One of the most memorable goals in the 2014 World Cup was scored by Robin van Persie in the Netherlands' 5–1 defeat of reigning champions Spain. The way his body moved as he lunged to head the goal was compared widely to which animal?**

    a) Dolphin ✓
    b) Eagle
    c) Elephant
    d) Snake

13. **Colombia borders four other countries in South America: Brazil, Venezuela, Ecuador and Peru. But against which other South American country did Colombian midfielder James Rodríguez score the goal of the 2014 World Cup: a chest-and-volley which flew in off the crossbar?**

    a) Argentina
    b) Chile
    c) Uruguay ✓
    d) Bolivia

14. **USA striker Carli Lloyd scored a hat-trick in the 2015 Women's World Cup final as her side beat Japan 5–2. What was spectacular about her third goal?**

    a) She scored from the halfway line. ✓
    b) She headed the ball in from outside the area.
    c) She scored from kick-off before Japan had touched the ball.
    d) She kicked the ball so hard that the net broke.

15. **Argentina's 3–2 win over West Germany at Mexico City's Estadio Azteca in the 1986 World Cup final was the highest-scoring final since 1970. What natural phenomena is Mexico City particularly at risk of?**

    a) Tsunamis
    b) Earthquakes ✓
    c) Footballs raining from the sky
    d) Avalanches

16. **What was controversial about England's third goal in the 1966 World Cup final, which put them 3–2 ahead against West Germany?**

    a) Three England players were offside at the time
    b) The West Germany goalkeeper was off the pitch injured
    c) The ball hit the crossbar and was ruled to have rebounded over the line before bouncing out ✓
    d) The referee wasn't sure if the ball had gone in, so asked the England fans behind the goal if he should allow it

17. **Which of the following vehicles is also a term used for a powerful shot?**

    a) Train   b) Rocket

    c) Tank   d) Bicycle

18. **One of the best team goals of all time was scored by Brazil against Italy in the 1970 World Cup. Brazil's players made twelve passes before captain Carlos Alberto Torres thundered the ball into the Italy goal. This goal is considered to be the perfect demonstration of the Brazilian style of playing, which Pelé called the "jogo bonito". What does this Portuguese phrase mean?**

    a) Bonny joggers
    b) The beautiful game ✓
    c) The ball jugglers
    d) Goals are fun

19. **What did Germany coach Joachim Löw say to Mario Götze during the extra-time break, before he scored the only goal of the 2014 World Cup final against Argentina?**

    a) "Whistle in their ears and distract their defenders!"

    b) "You are a miracle boy. Make it happen!"

    c) "Show to the world you are better than Messi and that you can decide the World Cup!"

    d) "Make them sweat, Super Mario!"

20. **What is the phrase that South American football commentators scream for as long as they can when a player scores a goal?**

    a) YEEEEESSSSSSSSSS!
    b) GOOAAAAALLLLLLL! ✓
    c) MAMMA MIAAAAAAA!
    d) OLÉ, OLÉ, OLÉÉÉÉÉ!

REFS AND RED CARDS

Rules. We may not like them but we all have to stick to them. Otherwise what would happen? Anarchy! Chaos! Meltdown! That's why referees are important in football. They keep the players in check – even if they sometimes make decisions that the fans don't agree with. A late penalty or controversial red card decision can even add to the drama of the game.

Originally referees only kept an eye on the time and each team had its own umpire, who would receive appeals from players if they felt a foul had been committed. Those discussions could take a long time, so in 1891, the referee was given power to make decisions on fouls and penalties. Two assistant referees, one on each side of the pitch, were on hand to help if required.

Referees need lots of pockets. They carry a yellow card, which they show to players if they make a bad tackle or behave rudely. They also have a red card, which is shown for a second yellow card or an offence such as a really dangerous tackle. They carry a notebook and pencil to jot down the names or numbers of players who receive the cards. And some referees even have a can of spray to mark out ten yards of space from where a free-kick is taken.

A referee's whistle is never far from their lips, so they can be heard above the noise of the game. Let's test the rules and find out what happens to the players who break them. Whistles at the ready... Peep! Peep!

1. **The role of the referee is to enforce the rules of football. These rules are set out in an important document called:**

   a) *Da Roolz*
   b) *The Book of Football Dos and Don'ts*
   c) *The Laws of the Game*
   d) *The Referee's Bible*

2. **Which item did referees use for the first time in 1878, in order to make games easier to control?**

   a) Whistle
   b) Megaphone
   c) Baton
   d) Whip

3. **The independent governing body that decides on the rules of football was set up in 1886 and is called the IFAB. What do the initials stand for?**

   a) Inhibiting Fouls Amid Ballgames
   b) International Fans of Alex and Ben
   c) International Football Association Board
   d) Incredibly Funny Assorted Ballplayers

4. Bolivian referee Ulises Saucedo was in charge of the 1930 World Cup match in which Argentina beat Mexico 6–3. What was his other job during the tournament?

a) Coach of Bolivia, who were also playing
b) Hairdresser to the FIFA president
c) Chef to the Bolivia delegation
d) President of Bolivia

5. The Battle of Santiago is the name given to the Chile v. Italy game in the 1962 World Cup because it was so violent. English referee Ken Aston sent off two players and armed police came onto the pitch three times to break up fights. What famous refereeing accessory did Aston invent a few years later?

a) Corner flag

b) Yellow and red cards

c) Small notebook

d) Vanishing spray

6. In the 1966 World Cup final, Tofiq Bahramov from Azerbaijan was the referee's assistant who ruled that Geoff Hurst's controversial shot had gone over the line to give England a crucial lead against West Germany. What building in Baku, the Azerbaijani capital, was named in his honour after his death in 1993?

a) The National Institute for the Blind
b) The Baku Courts of Justice
c) The country's favourite toffee factory
d) The national football stadium

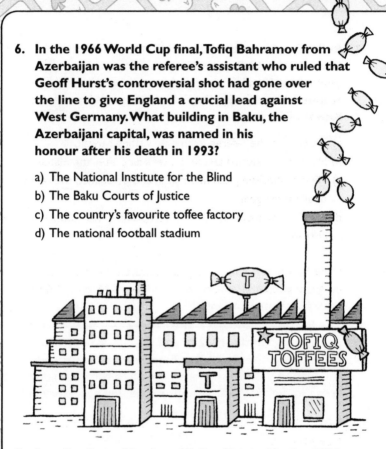

7. Israeli referee Abraham Klein officiated in the 1970, 1978 and 1982 World Cups, and is known as one of the best referees of all time. Why did he ask FIFA to miss some games during the 1982 World Cup in Spain?

a) His son was in the Israeli army fighting a war and he was too worried about him to concentrate on football.
b) He had a bad tummy after eating an uncooked burger.
c) He had lost his favourite whistle.
d) He injured his arm falling out of bed and couldn't raise it to show red or yellow cards.

8. **In the France v. Kuwait match in the first round of the 1982 World Cup, the referee awarded France a goal when Kuwait's players thought the game had stopped. How did Sheikh Fahad, the president of the Kuwaiti FA, react?**

   a) He banned the referee from ever visiting Kuwait.
   b) He threw a custard tart in the ref's face after the match.
   c) He ran onto the pitch mid-match and persuaded the ref to disallow the goal.
   d) He resigned from his position complaining that football was corrupt.

9. **How long did it take Uruguay defender José Batista to get a red card in record time in a 1986 World Cup match against Scotland?**

   a) 5 seconds
   b) 56 seconds
   c) 1 minute, 5 seconds
   d) 1 minute, 56 seconds

10. **Which is the correct referee sign for an indirect free kick?**

a)   b)   c)   d)

11. **Tunisian referee Ali Bin Nasser was in charge of the England v. Argentina quarter-final in the 1986 World Cup. The match is famous for being the game when Diego Maradona scored by punching the ball with his hand. This cheating move became known as the Hand of God, and along with his second goal, England were knocked out of the tournament. What excuse did Nasser give for missing the handball?**

a) The pea had fallen out of his whistle so he was not able to blow it.

b) He couldn't see because the sun was in his eyes and he wasn't allowed to wear sunglasses.

c) He said his assistant referee, Bulgarian Bogdan Dotchev, told him the goal was fine.

d) His sight was affected because he was taking medication for a sore bottom.

12. **What nickname did Dutch midfielder Frank Rijkaard earn for spitting in the hair of German striker Rudi Völler after they were both sent off in a grumpy game in the 1990 World Cup?**

a) Sir Saliva

b) Frankie the Spit

c) Llama

d) Walrus

13. How did England midfielder Paul Gascoigne react after being shown a yellow card in the 1990 World Cup semi-final against Germany?

a) He punched the referee.
b) He burst into tears.
c) He walked off the pitch as he thought it was a red.
d) He scored a hat-trick.

14. How many cards did referee Valentin Ivanov show at the 2006 World Cup game between Portugal and the Netherlands, which was nicknamed the Battle of Nuremberg?

a) 24 (18 yellow and 6 red)
b) 20 (16 yellow and 4 red)
c) 16 (13 yellow and 3 red)
d) 12 (2 yellow and 7 red)

15. Why did English referee Graham Poll go down in World Cup history in 2006?

a) He showed three yellow cards to the same player but didn't send him off.
b) He allowed a goal to stand after it had deflected off him.
c) He ran onto the pitch and celebrated when England scored a goal.
d) He showed an orange card when he wasn't sure if a player deserved a yellow or a red card.

16. **What did France captain Zinedine Zidane do to Italy defender Marco Materazzi that got him sent off in the 2006 World Cup final?**

a) He was sick on him.

b) He head-butted him.

c) He kissed him.

d) He tickled him.

17. **Why was Uruguay striker Luis Suárez sent off in the last minute of the 2010 World Cup quarter-final against Ghana?**

a) He saved a shot on the line with his hands.

b) He bit the ear of the Ghana goalkeeper.

c) He pulled down the referee's shorts.

d) He fought with his own coach.

18. **Bibiana Steinhaus, referee for the 2011 Women's World Cup final, made history in Germany in the 2017–18 season as the first female referee to take charge of men's top-flight games. What is her job when she is not on the pitch?**

a) Prison guard

b) Nursery teacher

c) Police officer

d) Driving instructor

19. **What nationality is Kharkiv-born Kateryna Monzul, who refereed the 2015 Women's World Cup final, in which USA beat Japan 5–2?**

a) Russian
b) Ukrainian
c) Japanese
d) American

20. **FIFA introduced technology called VAR in 2017 to help referees make the right decisions when it comes to allowing goals, awarding penalties and showing red cards. What does VAR stand for?**

a) Very Acrobatic Robots
b) Visual Approval Request
c) Video Assistant Referees
d) Value Analysis Report

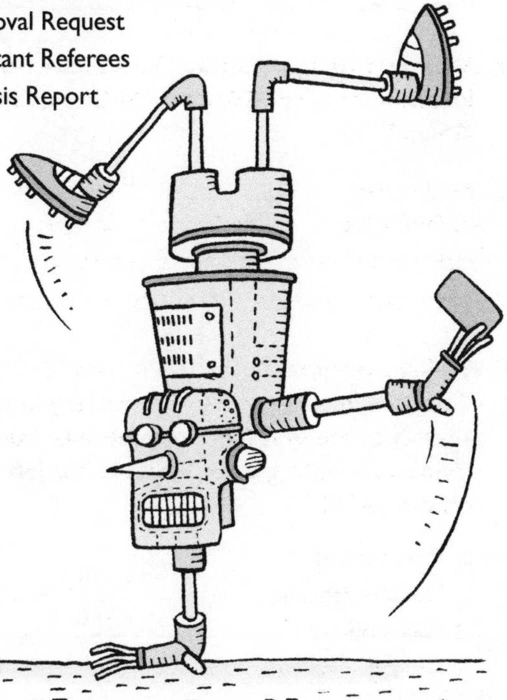

OUCHY INJURIES

Splat! Bang! Bump! Football is a contact sport, which means players often get hurt. Whether it's from accidental slips or nasty tackles, footballers inevitably score more bruises, sprains and knocks than goals. The tally of injuries in World Cups is always high, since the pressure on the players to win is so great. When you get the best players from around the world playing together in one competition, with the ultimate prize in reach, there can be painful consequences.

OWWW!

Most footballing injuries happen to the legs and feet, but the upper half of the body is also at risk, for example if you land badly on your wrist or back, or if you bang heads with an opponent. In this chapter we're going to look at some spectacular World Cup injuries and also learn about the body. Let's start at the top and work our way down. Now are you ready for your medical? Heads up!

1. **At the beginning of the 2014 World Cup final between Germany and Argentina, German midfielder Christoph Kramer received a knock to the head. He felt dazed and confused, so went up to the referee and asked:**

    a) "Ref, is this the final?"
    b) "Ref, what country am I in?"
    c) "Ref, what's my name?"
    d) "Ref, what's for tea?"

2. **Brandi Chastain scored the winning penalty in the 1999 Women's World Cup for USA. She has vowed to donate her brain for medical research purposes after her death. This is so scientists can learn more about the temporary brain injury players often get from a bump to the head – just like the one that happened to Christoph Kramer in the previous question. What is this injury known as?**

    a) Percussion
    b) Concussion
    c) Discussion
    d) Belarusian

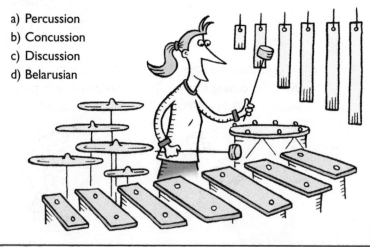

3. **One of the worst injuries ever to happen in an international game happened when West German keeper Harald Schumacher jumped for a high tackle against French forward Patrick Battiston in the 1982 World Cup semi-final. As well as being knocked unconscious, what other injuries did Battiston sustain?**

a) Lost one tooth, cracked four ribs
b) Lost two teeth, cracked three ribs
c) Lost three teeth, cracked two ribs
d) Lost four teeth, cracked one rib

4. **Scotland defender Kirk Broadfoot scored on his debut in a 2010 World Cup qualifier against Iceland. But what kitchen-related injury left him needing a hospital visit in 2009?**

a) He accidentally chopped off his hand when slicing a turnip.

b) An egg he had poached in his microwave blew up and squirted boiling water into his face.

c) He passed out because of the fumes coming from a mouldy haggis in his fridge.

d) Hiccups from drinking too much Irn-Bru triggered a mild heart attack.

5. **Why was Belgium captain Eric Gerets unhappy after his team drew 1–1 with Hungary in the 1982 World Cup?**

a) He was substituted after being accidentally knocked out by his own goalkeeper trying to block a cross.

b) He sprained his little finger during the pre-match handshake and had to be substituted.

c) He elbowed the referee by mistake and was sent off.

d) He was hit so hard on his bum by the ball that he couldn't sit down for 24 hours.

6. **Cristiano Ronaldo scored the winning penalty when Portugal beat England in the 2006 World Cup quarter-final. He also played in the 2010 and 2014 World Cups. The forward famously uses cryotherapy to speed up recovery and reduce injuries. What does it involve?**

a) Crying for three hours

b) Rubbing your body with an ointment made from the tears of a crocodile

c) Exposing your body to freezing cold temperatures for up to three minutes

d) Sleeping on a bed of nails once a week

7. **According to research by American scientists, are men or women more likely to pretend to be injured during football matches?**

a) There is no difference at all

b) Men are twice as likely to pretend

c) Women are twice as likely to pretend

d) Goalkeepers of both genders always pretend the most

8. **The human body contains 206 bones, including 54 in the hands and 52 in the feet. These bones are some of the ones that footballers fracture or injure most often. Can you identify them?**

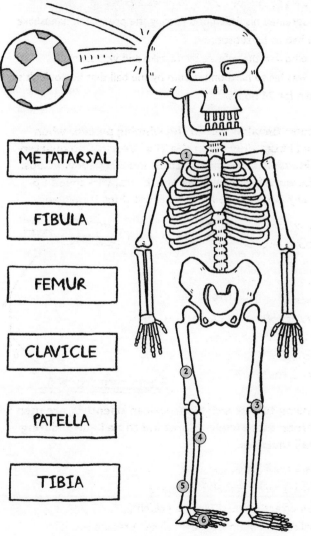

METATARSAL

FIBULA

FEMUR

CLAVICLE

PATELLA

TIBIA

9. **Midfielder Jean Beauséjour scored a stunning goal in Chile's 2014 World Cup win over Australia. Earlier in his career, Beauséjour witnessed one of the most gruesome injuries ever seen in a football stadium, which happened during the celebration for one of his goals. What was the injury and how did it happen?**

   a) A teammate broke his neck after somersaulting and falling awkwardly.

   b) A teammate, who went to celebrate with fans, had part of his finger torn off when his wedding ring got caught in the fence.

   c) A teammate was squashed to death when everyone piled on top him.

   d) The keeper of the opposite team kicked the post in frustration and snapped his leg.

10. **What did the Brazil team do at the beginning of their 2014 World Cup semi-final to mark the fact that their best player, Neymar, suffered a bad back injury in the previous match?**

    a) During the national anthem they held up a shirt with his name on it.

    b) They revealed that they all had "Neymar" tattooed on their left ankles.

    c) They changed their haircuts to look like Neymar's.

    d) They walked onto the pitch with a pet labradoodle called Neymar.

11. **Players including Víctor Valdés (Spain), Holger Badstuber (Germany), and England duo Theo Walcott and Jay Rodriguez missed the 2014 World Cup because of knee ligament injuries. Ligaments are cords inside the body that join bone to bone. What are the names of the ligaments in the knee, between the shin bone and the thigh bone, that many footballers tear and can take a year to heal?**

a) Crucial ligaments
b) Excruciating ligaments
c) Cruciate ligaments
d) Cruel ligaments

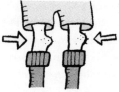

12. **How did Brazil striker Marta, named FIFA Women's World Player of the Year for five times in a row from 2006–2010, escape serious injury in December 2014?**

a) She lost control of her car and it went off the road, but she only ended up with a few bruises.
b) The rope snapped when she did a bungee jump, but she fell into some trees that broke her fall.
c) She was attacked by a crocodile in the Amazon rainforest, but kicked a ball in its mouth to stop it biting her.
d) She fell out of a boat, but was rescued by Neymar who happened to be windsurfing nearby.

13. **How is an injured player taken off the pitch when they are so hurt they cannot walk?**

   a) The doctor carries the injured player on their shoulders.
   b) Helpers carry the injured person on a stretcher.
   c) They are made to do a walking handstand off the pitch.
   d) Teammates roll the injured person to the touchline.

14. **Norway had a 56-year wait between appearing in two World Cups: the first in 1938 and the next in 1994. In the 1970s, Norway defender Svein Grøndalen played 77 times for his national team – but what reason did he give for missing an international match in 1980?**

   a) He strained his knee because the accelerator pedal in his new Ferrari was too far away.
   b) He slipped on a puddle of his dog's wee in his kitchen and tore a knee ligament.
   c) He was charged by a moose while out jogging and cut his leg running away from the beast.
   d) He caught hypothermia after falling into a river while out fishing with his nephew.

15. **Stars like Gareth Bale, Alexis Sánchez and Clint Dempsey use Kinesio Tape to reduce muscle pain and provide support for joints. It was invented by a Japanese doctor called Kenzo Kase in the 1970s. But what does using the tape involve?**

   a) Training with sticky-tape tied around both feet
   b) Singing a song called "Kinesio-o-o" in front of the whole team
   c) Sleeping with tape on the outermost bits of your body: nose, ears, elbows and toes
   d) Playing matches with thick tape strapped around a sore muscle

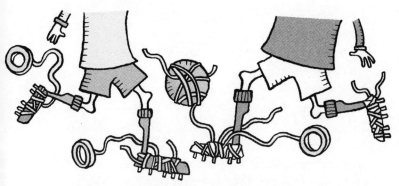

16. **Belgium striker Christian Benteke missed the 2014 World Cup after he injured his tendon. Tendons are pieces of tissue inside the body that attach muscle to bone. The tendon most vulnerable to footballing injuries is the one in the heel, which is named after a character from Greek myth. What is the tendon called?**

   a) The Achilles tendon
   b) The Hercules tendon
   c) The Medusa tendon
   d) The Zeus tendon

17. How did England team physio Gary Lewin make headlines at the 2014 World Cup?

a) He dropped the stretcher while trying to carry off an injured player.

b) He dislocated his ankle celebrating a goal by the touchline and had to be carried off on a stretcher.

c) He was blamed for giving the goalkeeper itchy socks to wear.

d) He caught a stomach bug and passed it on to the rest of the team.

18. Australia's Samantha Kerr is one of the best forwards in women's football. She made her first Australia appearance when she was only 15 and in 2017, aged 23, was nominated for the Best FIFA Women's Player award. She has recovered from many injuries, including two big knee injuries and foot ligament damage. How many different ligaments are there in the foot?

a) 3

b) 12

c) 28

d) 107

19. What was notable about the first ever World Cup match in 1930 when France beat Mexico 4–1?

a) France's goalkeeper Alex Thépot broke a toe by taking a goal-kick in the game; the wound later became infected and the toe was cut off.

b) France played with ten men for 80 minutes as their goalkeeper Alex Thépot went off injured and there were no substitutes.

c) France's main striker Lucien Laurent complained of heel blisters in the warm-up, so they borrowed one of Mexico's strikers for the match.

d) France's centre-forward André Maschinot scored two goals when playing with a broken leg.

20. How did Spain goalkeeper Santiago Cañizares rupture a tendon in his foot to make him miss the 2002 World Cup?

a) A glass bottle of aftershave shattered when he dropped it.

b) A dog bit him while he was out for a run.

c) He poured boiling water on it while making a cup of tea.

d) He got out of bed on the wrong side.

PRESSURE PENALTIES

There are two types of penalty in a World Cup. The first kind are awarded by referees during the game when there is a foul or handball committed in the penalty area. The second kind are taken during the penalty shoot-out, which you get when scores are level after extra-time during matches in the knock-out stage. In a shoot-out each team takes five kicks to decide the winner.

Penalty shoot-outs are one of the most exciting parts of the game and leave fans biting their nails in suspense. This is because the penalty-kick is football in its purest form: it's just the ball, a goal, one person shooting and a goalkeeper. It's what football is all about.

Focus!

If the shooter is good enough to be a professional footballer, let alone represent their country and play in a World Cup, then they should score from the penalty spot every time. But they don't. This is because the art of taking the perfect penalty is not just about having the right technique in your feet – you also need the right mindset in your brain.

Some of the best players in the world have missed important penalties in the World Cup because they were nervous, and pressure can affect performance. Taking on this chapter will be like a penalty shoot-out: you need to stay calm, not rush, keep focused and pick your spot carefully. Are you ready? Deep breath, and…

1. The first World Cup penalty kick was taken in the 1930 World Cup by Chile's Carlos Vidal, who had his effort saved by France goalkeeper Alex Thépot. The penalty had been around for a while before then – it was invented in 1891. In what country was the penalty invented?

    a) Hungary
    b) England
    c) Northern Ireland
    d) Egypt

2. What is the official name for a penalty taken during a penalty shoot-out, according to the FIFA rule book?

    a) Kicks from the penalty mark
    b) Shot from the spot
    c) Penalty-kick
    d) Hit and hope for the best

3. Who decides at which end of the pitch a penalty shoot-out takes place?

    a) The captain who wins the coin toss
    b) The captain who loses the coin toss
    c) The mascot who wins the coin toss
    d) The referee using a coin toss

4. **During a penalty shoot-out, where does the goalkeeper who is the teammate of the kicking player have to stand?**

   a) Anywhere outside the penalty area
   b) Outside the penalty area while still level with the goal line
   c) Behind the goal
   d) Anywhere the goalkeeper likes

5. **What is the distance from the penalty spot to the goal line?**

   a) 6 yards
   b) 12 yards
   c) 18 yards
   d) 30 yards

6. **Which Brazil player caused a change to FIFA rules in 2010 after he stopped in the middle of his run-up to make the goalkeeper dive first. Players are now allowed to slow down, but not stop their movement totally.**

   a) Pelé
   b) Neymar
   c) David Luiz
   d) Bellinhos

7. **What does West Germany midfielder Paul Breitner remember about scoring a penalty halfway through the first half of the 1974 World Cup final against the Netherlands, which his team went on to win 2–1?**

   a) Nothing at all because it was so stressful for him that he blocked it from his memory

   b) Telling the goalkeeper where he was going to kick his penalty

   c) Getting a nosebleed before he struck the ball

   d) Tripping over his shoelaces during his run-up

8. **What was special about the penalty that Germany defender Andreas Brehme scored to win the 1990 World Cup final against Argentina?**

   a) He had a broken shin-bone when he took it.

   b) He had lost both of his contact lenses earlier in the game.

   c) He pushed over his captain Lothar Matthäus in his desire to take the penalty.

   d) He struck it with his right foot; in the previous World Cup he scored a penalty struck with his left foot.

9. **West Germany won the first ever World Cup penalty shoot-out in the 1982 semi-final against France. One French player who missed was called Maxime Bossis. What was the name of the other player?**

   a) Didier Deux

   b) Didier Trois

   c) Didier Six

   d) Didier Dix

10. Who was the first team to win a World Cup final after a penalty shoot-out?

a) Uruguay in 1950
b) Brazil in 1994
c) Italy in 2006
d) Germany in 2014

11. What was Argentina goalkeeper Sergio Goycochea's good luck ritual that he claimed help win two penalty shoot-outs in the 1990 World Cup?

a) He weed in the goalmouth through his shorts.
b) He kissed both posts and the crossbar.
c) He didn't wear any pants.
d) He closed his eyes when he dived.

12. **How did Brandi Chastain celebrate scoring the winning penalty in a shoot-out for USA in the 1999 Women's World Cup final?**

   a) She swung from the crossbar of the goal.
   b) She did a handstand.
   c) She took off her top.
   d) She ran into the crowd to hug her mum.

13. **Which national team missed its first three penalties in a 2006 World Cup shoot-out, becoming the first team to lose a World Cup penalty shoot-out without managing to score a single penalty?**

   a) Ukraine
   b) Netherlands
   c) Switzerland
   d) England

14. **How did Italy midfielder Andrea Pirlo describe the walk from the centre-circle to the penalty spot before scoring in the 2006 World Cup final penalty shoot-out?**

   a) "A time when even my goosebumps had goosebumps."
   b) "An endless and terrible walk into one's own fears."
   c) "The most beautiful moment of my life."
   d) "The worst time ever to need the toilet."

15. What did Germany goalkeeper Jens Lehmann take out of his sock to help him win a penalty shoot-out against Argentina in the 2006 World Cup?

a) A piece of paper telling him where the opposition liked to kick their penalties

b) A new set of gloves

c) A stink bomb

d) A lucky stick of chewing-gum

16. Why was Japan goalkeeper Ayumi Kaihori the hero when Japan beat USA after a penalty shoot-out in the 2011 Women's World Cup final?

a) She saved two penalties in the shoot-out.

b) She scored the penalty to win the game.

c) She broke her hand earlier in the game but kept playing.

d) She lost the sight in one eye, as a bird pooed on her face just before the final penalty.

17. **How did Netherlands coach Louis van Gaal use mind games to affect the opposing Costa Rica players before a penalty shoot-out in the 2014 World Cup?**

   a) He told all the Costa Rica players that they would miss their penalties.
   b) He sang the Dutch national anthem as loudly as he could.
   c) He brought on a substitute goalkeeper for the shoot-out.
   d) He pulled down his trousers when Costa Rica players were shooting.

18. **Which national team has the worst record in penalty shoot-outs in major international tournaments, including World Cups?**

   a) Nigeria
   b) France
   c) Mexico
   d) England

19. What unites international legends Diego Maradona (Argentina), Roberto Baggio (Italy) and Andriy Shevchenko (Ukraine)?

a) They all scored penalties in a World Cup final.
b) They all scored a hat-trick of penalties for their national team.
c) They all missed penalties in World Cup penalty shoot-outs.
d) They all missed five penalties in a row.

20. The word penalty comes from the Latin word *poena*, which means:

a) Poem
b) Punishment
c) Poo
d) Pony

SHOCK RESULTS

Life is unpredictable. You never know what's going to happen next – that's why it can be so fun! Football is also unpredictable. One of the most exciting things about the game is that sometimes the underdog wins. These upsets teach us two great lessons in life: never give up in the face of a tough challenge and don't be complacent or over-confident if you think something will be easy. Whatever the task, you always have to give your best – that way, you can have no complaints about the result.

World Cups always throw up a few surprises. Sometimes the national team of a tiny country beats a bigger country, or (as has happened to England in the past) a team with amateur players beats a professional team. Here we are going to relive some of the biggest upsets in international football. They are what make football so exhilarating. Are you sitting on the edge of your seat?

1. One of the greatest World Cup shocks was in 1950 in Brazil. England were expected to win the tournament and had some of the world's most famous players. The second team they faced, USA, was made up of amateurs, which means the players were not professionals but had other jobs, including a postman and a funeral car driver. USA won 1–0. What was special about the USA goalscorer, Joe Gaetjens, whose job was washing dishes in a restaurant?

   a) He was not an American citizen, but was from Haiti, a Caribbean island about 600 miles from Miami.
   b) At 6ft 8ins, he was the tallest ever World Cup goalscorer.
   c) He went on to invent the modern dishwasher.
   d) His real name was Joe Bloggs.

2. **Hosts Brazil also unexpectedly lost 2–1 in the 1950 World Cup final against arch-rivals Uruguay, a result that historians describe as the greatest tragedy in Brazilian history. Brazil's keeper, Barbosa, was blamed for the defeat in front of nearly 200,000 fans and for the rest of his life people treated him as an outcast. What did he reportedly do many years later to help him get over the defeat?**

a) He appeared on Brazil's most popular reality TV show.

b) He burned the goalposts from the 1950 World Cup final on a barbecue.

c) He wrote and recorded a song called "Desculpa", meaning "Sorry", which got to number one.

d) He went to live in Uruguay.

3. **Hungary showed they were a team to watch when they beat England 6–3 at Wembley in 1953. They quickly became known as the Golden Team. In the group stage of the 1954 World Cup, Hungary then beat West Germany 8–3. The two teams met again in the final. Hungary were 2–0 ahead after ten minutes but then lost 3–2. What did the game become known as?**

a) The Miracle of Bern

b) The Shock of Basel

c) The Surprise of Zurich

d) The Jolt of Geneva

4. In the 1962 World Cup, the Chilean team used a tasty tactic in their preparations. Before each match, they would have some food or drink from the national cuisine of their opponents. And this plan seemed to work. They beat Switzerland, former champions Italy and the formidable USSR (as Russia used to be known).

What did they have before the Switzerland game?

a) Swiss chocolate

b) Swiss cheese

c) Muesli

d) Swiss roll

What did they have before the Italy game?

a) Spaghetti

b) Pizza

c) Risotto

d) Tiramisu

What did they have before the Russia game?

a) Caviar

b) Beetroot soup

c) Potato salad

d) Vodka

5. North Korea was the only team representing Asia and Africa at the 1966 World Cup hosted by England. They had never played in a World Cup before and were expected to lose heavily. But they won their final group match against Italy 1–0 in Middlesbrough. How did the players warm up for that game?

a) By wearing red, the same colour as local club Middlesbrough so the fans would like them

b) Singing patriotic songs at full volume on the train from London to Middlesbrough

c) Learning Italian to confuse their opponents

d) Practising with ping-pong balls so it would seem easier when they played with a bigger ball

6. Italy's defeat by North Korea knocked them out of the 1966 World Cup. Who, or what, greeted the Italy players when they came home?

a) Italian president Giuseppe Saragat with medals of dishonour

b) Fans throwing rotten fruit at them

c) The players' wives ready to join them on a flight to Greece to escape angry fans

d) The ambassador to North Korea

7. **Coach Ally MacLeod took one of the strongest ever Scotland sides to the 1978 World Cup in Argentina. He told fans that Scotland could reach the semi-finals, but they failed to get out of their group, after losing their opening match to which South American country?**

a) COLOMBIA

b) ECUADOR

c) PERU

d) BOLIVIA

8. **Before Algeria beat West Germany in a match of the 1982 World Cup, they were described as "minnows". This term is often used to describe teams from smaller countries at a World Cup. What is a minnow?**

a) A flea   b) A fish   c) A mouse   d) A squirrel

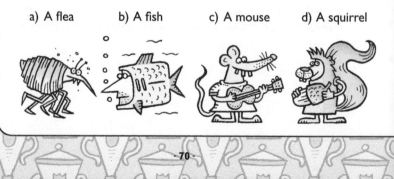

9. **Before Iceland qualified for the 2018 World Cup, the smallest country by population to play in the World Cup appeared in 1982 and beat hosts Spain to top their group. Who were they?**

a) Bolivia
b) Costa Rica
c) New Zealand
d) Northern Ireland

10. **El Salvador lost 10–1 to Hungary in their first match at the 1982 World Cup in Spain. How did El Salvador rebuild their confidence in preparation for playing Belgium and Argentina?**

a) They spent three days in a waterpark on Spain's east coast and did not mention football.
b) They played against the waiters in their hotel and beat them easily.
c) Their wives and families arrived to make them feel less homesick.
d) They did extra shooting after the match and allowed fans to join in.

11. **Coach Valery Nepomnyashchy led Cameroon to the 1990 World Cup quarter-finals, beating an Argentina side that included Diego Maradona on the way. Prior to this success, in what league did he have his only season as a club coach?**

a) English first division
b) Cameroonian second division
c) Japanese first division
d) Russian second division

12. **The phrase "an underdog" is often used to describe a team not expected to win a match, such as when Bulgaria beat Germany in the 1994 World Cup quarter-final. This term was first used in the nineteenth century, originating from which of these activities?**

   a) Dog fighting. The dog expected to win was the top dog.
   b) Dog racing. The most timid dog would sit under the starter's chair.
   c) Dog flying. The weakest dogs always flew the lowest.
   d) Dog selling. Some scrawny dogs sold for less than the registered price.

13. **How did the owner of Italian club Perugia respond when his South Korea player, Ahn Jung-Hwan, scored the goal that knocked Italy out of the 2002 World Cup?**

   a) He doubled his salary and made him captain.
   b) He sacked him.
   c) He changed the team name to FC Hwan.
   d) He made every player have a Hwan haircut.

14. **Dakar is the capital city of which African nation that beat defending champions France in the opening match of the 2002 World Cup, which was one of the biggest shocks of the tournament?**

    a) Egypt
    b) Ghana
    c) Senegal
    d) Ivory Coast

15. **Why are the final games in the first round groups in knock-out competitions like the World Cup played at the same time?**

    a) To avoid two teams fixing a result to ensure they both go through
    b) To get to the end of the tournament quicker
    c) To make it more exciting for fans with two TV sets
    d) So the players don't have to go to bed too late

16. **Brazil stunned USA in the 2007 Women's World Cup semi-final, winning 4–0. Their win ended a three-year unbeaten run for USA that had lasted for how many matches?**

    a) 38
    b) 51
    c) 76
    d) 108

17. **New Zealand were playing in only their second World Cup in 2010 when they drew 1–1 with current champions Italy in the group stages. They even had an amateur player, who worked in a bank, in their side. What was surprising about the way New Zealand left the tournament?**

   a) They were unbeaten as they also drew with Slovakia and Paraguay, but didn't earn enough points to get through.
   b) They were unable to play their final game as a herd of sheep had escaped onto the pitch and could not be moved.
   c) Coach Ricki Herbert picked himself to play in goal but conceded eight goals to Paraguay.
   d) The banker was sent off after offering the referee chocolate money.

18. **What was especially curious about the Spain v. Netherlands match in the 2014 World Cup, which the Dutch surprised everyone by winning 5-1?**

   a) It was the first time a World Cup match kicked off at breakfast local time.
   b) It was the first time that the two finalists from a previous World Cup were drawn against each other in their first games of the following World Cup.
   c) It was the first ever World Cup match in an indoor stadium.
   d) It was the first ever World Cup match where ten of the players on the pitch shared the same birthday.

19. USA beat Japan 5–2 in a thrilling 2015 Women's World Cup final. What was the score after 17 minutes of the game?

a) USA 0 Japan 0

b) USA 2 Japan 2

c) USA 0 Japan 2

d) USA 4 Japan 0

20. Match the flags to the World Cup teams responsible for some of the biggest shocks in the competition.

a) USA 1950   b) North Korea 1966

c) Cameroon 1990   d) Bulgaria 1994

e) Senegal 2002   f) New Zealand 2010

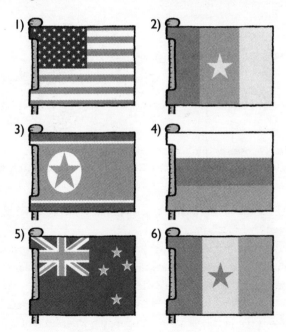

MIGHTY MASCOTS

Every World Cup since 1966 has had a mascot, a lovable character that is the symbol of that competition and the host nation. Mascots can be animals, children, fruit, objects and made-up or imaginary characters. At the beginning of each World Cup match, you normally see someone in a mascot costume fooling about on the pitch – just like you see club mascots waving to fans before league games. Fans love mascots because they are cute or hilarious, and add to the playful and fun atmosphere.

We also like mascots because they teach us something about our World Cup hosts. Mascots often represent something important from that country, perhaps an animal that lives there, a child wearing traditional clothes or a fruit that the country is famous for. Not only do mascots celebrate football, but they celebrate the cultural heritage of different countries.

The word mascot comes from the French word *mascotte*, which means "lucky charm". You'll need the best of luck to answer these questions!

1. **The first ever World Cup mascot was created for the 1966 World Cup in England. What was his name and what animal was he?**

   a) World Cup Willie   b) World Cup Winston   c) World Cup Wayne   d) World Cup Warren

2. **Which one of these things does a mascot do?**

   a) Appears on the pitch at the start of matches
   b) Cooks snacks for fans to eat at half-time
   c) Plays as a substitute for the home team
   d) Checks tickets to allow fans into the ground

3. **The 1970 World Cup mascot was a boy called Juanito, who wore a Mexico kit and which type of hat?**

   a) Sombrero   b) Boater

   c) Deerstalker   d) Top hat

4. **The mascots for the 1974 World Cup in West Germany were two boys in West Germany kit called:**

   a) Yin and Yang
   b) Tip and Tap
   c) Klopp and Löw
   d) Wurst and Pretzel

5. **The mascot for the 1978 World Cup in Argentina was called Gauchito, which means "Little Gaucho" in Spanish. Gauchos are the horsemen who herd cattle on the grasslands of Argentina. What three accessories did Gauchito have?**

   a) Neckerchief, whip, wide-brimmed hat
   b) Horse, saddle and helmet
   c) Water pistol, lasso and holster
   d) Spurs, whisky bottle, poncho

6. **Which fruit, one of Spain's main food exports, was Naranjito, the mascot of the 1982 World Cup in Spain?**

   a) A lemon

   b) A melon

   c) An orange

   d) A strawberry

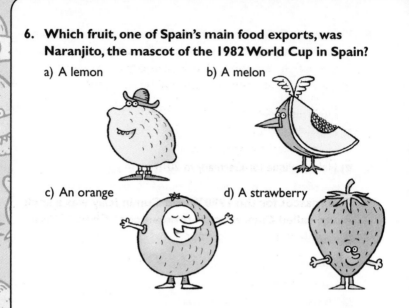

7. **What object was Pique, the mascot for the 1986 World Cup in Mexico?**

   a) A rattlesnake
   b) A green jalapeño pepper
   c) A cactus
   d) A taco

8. The name Pique was a good choice for a World Cup mascot because, in a later World Cup, a player called Piqué was in the team that won the tournament! Who was he and which team did he play for?

    a) Emmanuel Piqué for France in 1998
    b) Ronaldinho Piqué for Brazil in 2002
    c) Gerard Piqué for Spain in 2010
    d) Helmut Piqué for Germany in 2014

9. The mascot for the 1990 World Cup in Italy was a stick figure called Ciao, which is pronounced "Chow". What does "ciao" mean in Italian?

    a) "Hello!"
    b) "Goodbye!"
    c) "Goal!"
    d) It can mean both "Hello!" and "Goodbye!"

10. What was the name of the puppy who was the mascot for the 1994 World Cup in USA?

    a) Striker
    b) Washington
    c) Soccer Dawg
    d) Brave

11. **Footix was the name of the mascot for the 1998 World Cup in France. Which animal, one of France's national symbols, was he?**

a) Frog
b) Cockerel
c) Bear
d) Fox

12. **What was the name of the fox who was the mascot for the 1999 Women's World Cup in USA?**

a) Foxy
b) Roxy
c) Nutmeg
d) Vulpie

13. **How many mascots were there for the 2002 World Cup in Japan and South Korea? The mascots were collectively known as the Spheriks.**

a) 2
b) 3
c) 4
d) 5

14. **A teacher, who was inspired by an ancient tale, designed the mascot for the 2003 Women's World Cup chosen hosts China. What was the name of the mascot?**

a) Famous Lady
b) Warrior Striker
c) Ancient Girl
d) She didn't have a name

15. **The mascots for the 2006 World Cup in Germany were a lion called Goleo VI, and Pille, who was a talking what?**

a) Whistle

b) Ball

c) World

d) Boot

* a) Peep!   b) Bounce!   c) Turn!   d) Shoot!

16. **Zakumi, the mascot for the 2010 World Cup in South Africa, was which animal common to that country?**

   a) Lion
   b) Giraffe
   c) Leopard
   d) Elephant

17. **What was the name of the cat who was the mascot for the 2011 Women's World Cup hosted in Germany?**

   a) Karla Kick
   b) Greta Goalpost
   c) Halle Hat-Trick
   d) Brenda Ball

18. **One of the reasons that Brazil chose a three-banded armadillo as its mascot for the 2014 World Cup was to let people know that it is an endangered species. What other ball-related reason made it a good choice for the competition?**

   a) Its nose is a ball shape.
   b) It mashes its food into balls before eating it.
   c) Its poo is the shape of a football.
   d) When scared it protects itself by curling up into a ball.

19. **What type of bird, common to host country Canada, was Shuéme, the mascot for the 2015 Women's World Cup? The mascot was inspired by the word "chouette", which is the French name for this animal.**

    a) Great white owl
    b) Pied kingfisher
    c) Toco toucan
    d) Lovebird parrot

20. **Zabivaka, the 2018 World Cup mascot, means "goalscorer" in Russian. What animal is he?**

    a) Polar bear

    b) Lynx

    c) Woolly mammoth

    d) Wolf

JEEPERS KEEPERS

Imagine you're a goalkeeper. It's the World Cup final, the opposition team has a penalty and the only thing stopping their victory is … you. You dive the right way, save the penalty and become a hero! Hurrah! The goalkeeper is an important and unique part of any football team. They are there to stop the very thing that we all want to see in football: goals. And that's why it's got to be one of the toughest position on the pitch.

A goalkeeper needs to be calm under pressure, because one silly mistake can lose a game. A strong goalkeeper makes the whole team feel secure.

Goalkeepers have a few things in common: they take on responsibilities that the other players don't have and when they save the ball, they save the whole team. The goalkeeper is also often the odd one out: the only player who can handle the ball, the only one with padded gloves and they even wear a different colour shirt to their teammates.

Sometimes the keeper is odd in other ways too. There are many cases of colourful and eccentric wearers of the Number 1 shirt. We'll meet some of them here. So get your gloves on and get ready to save the day!

1. **Ricardo Zamora represented Spain between 1920 and 1936 and is one of the few players to have played for both Real Madrid and Barcelona. The prize now given to the La Liga goalkeeper who concedes the fewest goals is called the Zamora Trophy. What new style of save did Zamora invent, which became known as a Zamorana?**

a) Letting the ball hit the face to stop it

b) Bouncing off a post to get more spring to dive across the goal

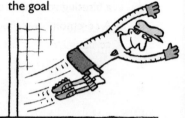

c) Diving at the striker's feet before they could shoot

d) Punching the ball away with the forearms or elbows

2. **Goalkeepers Gianpiero Combi and Dino Zoff captained Italy to World Cup success in 1934 and 1982 respectively. Who is the only other goalkeeper to have won the World Cup as captain?**

a) Fabien Barthez (France 1998)

b) Oliver Kahn (Germany 2002)

c) Iker Casillas (Spain 2010)

d) Manuel Neuer (Germany 2014)

3. In football, the word "scapegoat" is used to describe a person who gets the blame (usually unfairly) for a team defeat, such as Brazil goalkeeper Barbosa who was blamed for conceding two goals in the 1950 World Cup final. Where does the meaning of the word come from?

   a) The German goat Hennes, the mascot of German club Cologne, who once distracted the team's goalkeeper
   b) It's a phrase from Italian opera, where a singer who sings like a bleating goat ruins the entire performance.
   c) A ceremony described in the Bible in which all the sins of a community are transferred onto a goat. The goat is then sent into the wilderness.
   d) In the ancient Olympic Games, the athlete who finished last in a race was given a sack of goat poo.

4. What was the nickname of Julio Musimessi, one of the goalkeepers in Argentina's 1958 World Cup squad, and wrongly assumed to be the grandfather of Lionel Messi?

   a) The Singer Goalkeeper
   b) The Legend's Grandpa
   c) The Catching Cat
   d) Jumping Julio

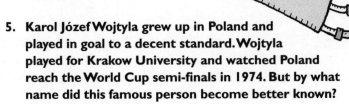

5. Karol Józef Wojtyla grew up in Poland and played in goal to a decent standard. Wojtyla played for Krakow University and watched Poland reach the World Cup semi-finals in 1974. But by what name did this famous person become better known?

   a) Caroline Wozniacki
   b) Pope John Paul II
   c) Joe Hart
   d) Jo Nesbø

6. **In the 1974 World Cup, Netherlands keeper Jan Jongbloed conceded only one goal in the six games that led his team to the final of the tournament. It made him a hero in his country, and when the tournament was over Ajax, one of the biggest Dutch teams, tried to sign him. Why did he refuse?**

   a) He grew up as a fan of Ajax's biggest rivals Feyenoord.
   b) He was not prepared to give up his weekly day off spent fishing.
   c) He did not get on well with Ajax star Johan Cruyff.
   d) He was allergic to the new grass installed at the Ajax training ground.

7. **Goalkeeper Peter Shilton played 125 times for England, including the 1982, 1986 and 1990 World Cups. How did he try to improve his reach for high crosses?**

   a) He hung from a balcony with weights attached to his feet in the hope it would help him grow.
   b) He lifted his arms above his head for five hours a day.
   c) He slept standing up
   d) He spent six hours every day on a trampoline.

8. With long black curly hair and a thick moustache, Colombia goalkeeper René Higuita was one of the most recognizable footballers of the 1990s. He was also nicknamed *El Loco*, the Madman, because of his high risk, flamboyant style. He played in the 1990 World Cup, but one of his most famous saves came after that, when he blocked a ball from England's Jamie Redknapp by diving forwards and clearing the ball with his heels. What was this save called?

a) The René Bounce
b) The Scorpion Kick
c) The Higuita Feeter
d) The Heel of God

9. The only World Cup final to finish 0–0 was played between Italy and Brazil in 1994. What are goalkeepers said to keep after not conceding a goal?

a) A straight face
b) A blank canvas
c) A clean sheet
d) A shut door

10. How did Mexico goalkeeper Jorge Campos contribute to his 1994 World Cup squad?

a) He designed the colourful goalkeeper shirt that he wore at the tournament.
b) He cooked stew for the squad every night using his grandma's secret recipe.
c) He sang opera to the team at half-time to relax their mind.
d) He was the coach as well as the goalkeeper.

11. **What surprising item did goalkeeper Boris Mihaylov wear while playing for Bulgaria in the 1994 World Cup?**

a) A wig
b) An eye-patch
c) Shoulder-pads
d) A cape

12. **Which of the following has German goalkeeper Jens Lehmann NOT done?**

a) Been sent off in a Champions League final
b) Weed behind the goal during a Champions League game
c) Been accused of theft after snatching a fan's glasses off his face and walking away from him
d) Won the World Cup

13. **During the 1998 World Cup in France, the French keeper Fabien Barthez was part of a very strange pre-match superstition that led his country all the way to the title. What was it?**

a) Defender Laurent Blanc would kiss his bald head just before kick-off.
b) He would hug the referee in the tunnel.
c) He would hang from the crossbar for a minute before kick-off with his left hand.
d) He would dance a jive with defender Lilian Thuram in the dressing-room.

14. **José Luis Chilavert is Paraguay's best goalkeeper of all time, playing for them in both the 1998 and 2002 World Cups. He was good at saving – and taking – penalties. Indeed, he scored a penalty on his debut for Paraguay in a World Cup qualifying match. He also had a reputation for a fiery temper. What was his nickname?**

a) Bulldog

b) Crocodile

c) Bear

d) Puppy

15. **Goalkeeper Rogério Ceni, who was part of Brazil's 2002 World Cup winning squad, holds the record for the most appearances for a single club (1,250 times for São Paulo). What other record does he hold?**

a) The only keeper to eat his gloves on the pitch
b) The most number of goals ever scored by a goalkeeper
c) The only keeper to score a World Cup hat-trick
d) The first goalkeeper to swim the length of the Amazon river

16. **Gigi Buffon – a member of Italy's 2006 World Cup winning team – decided to become a goalkeeper when, aged 14 years old, he saw a player make amazing saves in the 1990 World Cup. Buffon was so inspired by this keeper that when his son was born many years later, he named him after that player. Who was he?**

a) Walter Zenga (Italy)
b) Thomas N'Kono (Cameroon)
c) Peter Shilton (England)
d) Sergio Goycochea (Argentina)

17. **Germany goalkeeper Nadine Angerer saved a penalty from Brazil forward Marta to help her country win the 2007 Women's World Cup final 2–0. How many goals did Angerer concede in her six games in the competition?**

a) Zero
b) Three
c) Six
d) Twelve

18. **What was memorable about the winners' medal that goalkeeper Andrés Palop took home when Spain won the 2008 European Championship?**

a) He melted it down and made it into a ring for his wife.
b) He never made an appearance for Spain.
c) The medal said "Congratulations on winning the World Cup" by mistake.
d) He played as a striker despite being a goalkeeper.

19. Which female American goalkeeper became the first in USA history to keep 100 clean sheets in international matches after a 1–0 win in 2016?

a) Megan Rapinoe
b) Hope Solo
c) Alex Morgan
d) Carli Lloyd

20. The famous French thinker Albert Camus was also a talented goalkeeper in his youth. Which of the following sentences did he write?

a) "I quickly learned that the ball never came to you where you expected it. This helped me in life ... where people are not wholly straightforward."

b) "A goalkeeper is like a pain au chocolat in a bag of croissants."

c) "Je suis numero un!"

d) "I save therefore I am."

HAPPY FAMILIES

At Football School we believe that family is the most important thing in the world. But football comes a close second! We love playing football with members of our family, so imagine how fun it would be to play professional football with or against your sibling, or even a parent? It would be a thrilling mix of competitive spirit and pride.

Incredibly, five sets of brothers – including one set of twins, the Dutch duo René and Willy Van de Kerkhof in 1978 – have played in the biggest match of all: the World

Cup final. In this chapter, we'll meet some talented brothers and sisters who have been on the ball ever since they grew up together. A player's talent comes from a combination of nurture (their environment) and nature (the genes that they inherit from their parents). Oh brother! The players in this chapter certainly got an advantage from their family tree. Now, are you ready for our mother of all quizzes that celebrates footballing families from around the world?

1. Solve this riddle. What relation to Cristiano Ronaldo is his brother's sister's mother?

   a) Cousin
   b) Sister
   c) Mother
   d) Aunt

2. Incredibly more than 50 sets of brothers have been selected in World Cup squads since 1930. But there has been only one set of THREE brothers in the same squad. Who were they and which country did they represent?

   a) Palacios brothers from Honduras (2010)
   b) Kovač brothers from Croatia (2002)
   c) Koeman brothers from the Netherlands (1990)
   d) Charlton brothers from England (1966)

3. Tomás Balcázar, who played in the 1954 World Cup, is the only player whose grandson has also played in a World Cup. Who is his grandson?

   a) Javier Hernández (Mexico)
   b) Lionel Messi (Argentina)
   c) Alexis Sánchez (Chile)
   d) David Luiz (Brazil)

4. **Twins Helmut and Erwin Kremers played for the same three German clubs in their careers. Erwin helped West Germany in Euro 1972, while Helmut was in the squad that won the 1974 World Cup. But what did they do when they stopped playing football?**

a) They starred in a play together called *The Goal of My Dreams*

b) They set up a farm called The Goat of My Dreams

c) They released a pop song called "The Girl of My Dreams"

d) They set up a dream-interpreting service called The Dream of my Dreams

5. **Abedi Pele won the African Cup of Nations for Ghana in 1982, the Champions League with Marseille in 1993 and three African Footballer of the Year titles. What are the names of his children, who were in Ghana's 2014 World Cup squad?**

a) Jordan and André Ayew

b) Baffour and Asamoah Gyan

c) Kwesi and Stephen Appiah

d) Billy and John Boye

6. **How did former Belgium goalkeeper Jean-Marie Pfaff, a semi-finalist in the 1986 World Cup, become famous after he retired?**

a) He became a TV star in a reality show following his family every day for over ten years.

b) He sang in a pop group with his three daughters.

c) He was elected Belgian prime minister and appointed his wife as deputy.

d) He starred in an advert for milk with his parents.

7. **Brazil midfielder Bebeto famously celebrated scoring against the Netherlands in the 1994 World Cup quarter-final by rocking an imaginary baby, alongside teammates Romário and Mazinho, to commemorate the birth of his son. Mazinho already had two sons, Thiago and Rafinha, but how did they go on to become famous in football?**

a) They invented a self-lacing football boot called the Mazinhator.

b) They both won the Spanish league with Barcelona before Thiago chose to play for Spain and Rafinha for Brazil.

c) They set up a team in Brazil called Mazinho FC, that won the Brazilian league.

d) They changed their names to Thi Von Ago and Raf Van Inha and became Dutch citizens.

8. **Which pair of identical twins was the first to both score a goal at a World Cup?**

   a) René and Willy Van de Kerkhof of the Netherlands (Argentina 1978)

   b) Hossam and Ibrahim Hassan of Egypt (Italy 1990)

   c) Frank and Ronald de Boer of the Netherlands, (France 1998)

   d) Vasili and Aleksei Berezutski of Russia (Brazil 2014)

9. **Brothers Michael and Brian Laudrup, two of the best players in Denmark's football history, played together at the 1998 World Cup. What was the name of their father, who also played for Denmark?**

   a) Funn

   b) Fann

   c) Finn

   d) Fenn

10. **There have been six coaches who picked their own sons in their World Cup squad. Which father-and-son combination went furthest in the tournament, reaching the quarter-finals?**

a) Cesare and Paolo Maldini (Italy 1998)
b) Zlatko and Niko Kranjčar (Croatia 2006)
c) Ilija and Dušan Petković (Serbia and Montenegro 2006)
d) Bob and Michael Bradley (USA 2010)

11. **Slovakia winger Vladimír Weiss was coached at the 2010 World Cup by his dad Vladimír Weiss. His granddad was also a professional footballer, who played for Czechoslovakia (which Slovakia used to be part of). What was his name?**

a) Adel Weiss
b) Ice Weiss
c) Thrice Weiss
d) Vladimír Weiss

12. **How did Bára Skaale Klakstein and her daughter Eydvør make history in the Faroe Islands women's team 6–0 victory over Luxembourg in 2012? It was a friendly match before the team's first entry into qualification for the 2015 World Cup.**

a) They were joint coaches of the Faroes team.
b) Bára played for the Faroes and Eydvør for Luxembourg.
c) They became the first parent-child combination to play for the same international team.
d) Bára was the referee, but she got injured and was replaced by Eydvør.

13. **What was unique about the 2010 World Cup game between Germany and Ghana in which brothers Jérôme and Kevin-Prince Boateng played?**

   a) The brothers were playing for different countries
   b) The brothers both scored own goals
   c) The brothers were both sent off
   d) The brothers' uncle, Bobby Boateng, was the referee

14. **Which set of brothers was part of Ivory Coast's 2014 World Cup squad?**

   a) Yaya and Kolo Touré
   b) Thierno and Boubacar Barry
   c) Bonaventure and Salomon Kalou
   d) Serge Aurier and Wilfried Bony

15. **What was the relationship between Colombia players James Rodríguez and David Ospina at the 2014 World Cup?**

   a) Brothers-in-law
   b) Second cousins
   c) Uncle and nephew
   d) Husband and husband

16. **Belgium winger Eden Hazard, who played in the 2014 World Cup, has three brothers who are all talented footballers. His parents Thierry and Carine both played to a high standard, but what positions did they play?**

a) Winger (Thierry) and winger (Carine)
b) Goalkeeper (Thierry) and striker (Carine)
c) Centre-back (Thierry) and full-back (Carine)
d) Midfielder (Thierry) and forward (Carine)

17. **How is forward Sydney Leroux, part of USA's 2015 Women's World Cup winning side, related to American international footballer Dom Dwyer?**

a) Sister
b) Wife
c) Cousin
d) Mother

18. **How did Belgium midfielder Radja Nainggolan make history with his sister, attacking midfielder Riana Nainggolan, in 2015?**

a) They made their World Cup debuts for Belgium men's and women's teams on the same day.
b) They became the first set of twins to play for the men's and the women's teams of the same top tier club, Roma.
c) They were both elected to the Belgian parliament.
d) They entered Wimbledon as a mixed doubles pair.

19. **Three generations of the Forsberg family from Sweden became professional footballers: Lennart, who made his debut in the 1950s, was nicknamed Foppa. His son, Leif, who played in the 1980s and 1990s, was nicknamed Lill-Foppa, meaning Little Foppa. What is the nickname of Leif's son Emil, a winger who plays for the national team?**

   a) Flipper-Foppa
   b) Nano-Foppa
   c) Mini-Foppa
   d) Baby-Foppa

20. **Björn Sigurðarson scored Iceland's goal against Kosovo that qualified the team for the 2018 World Cup, its first ever World Cup appearance. What impressive feat was achieved by his mother, Bjarney Johannesdottir?**

   a) She also scored for Iceland in a Women's World Cup qualifier.
   b) She has three other sons who have all scored for the Iceland national team.
   c) She was coach of Iceland at the time.
   d) She is Iceland's prime minister.

That's my mum!

RECORD BREAKERS

The World Cup is a record breaker: the tournament is the most watched football competition in the sporting calendar, and the final is probably the most watched single sporting event in the world. In 2014, more than a billion television viewers watched at least some of the final in Brazil.

The World Cup is also a platform for record breakers. In this chapter, we are looking at those individual players and teams who have achieved things that no one

else has. Among our record breakers, we'll be meeting the top goal-scorers, and discovering the highest audiences and the biggest scorelines.

Imagine how it feels to be a record breaker. We think our pupils at Football School are the best of the best of the best, so we want you to aim high. Top of the class, everyone!

1. Australia's 31–0 defeat of American Samoa in a World Cup qualifier in 2001 set the record for the largest ever margin of victory in an international football match. How many goals did Australia striker Archie Thompson score?

   a) 0
   b) 6
   c) 13
   d) 20

2. Alberto Suppici was the youngest coach to lift the World Cup. How old was he when Uruguay won the first ever World Cup in 1930?

   a) 19
   b) 26
   c) 31
   d) 33

3. What prize did France striker Just Fontaine receive for scoring a record 13 goals at the 1958 World Cup?

   a) A boot made of gold
   b) An air rifle
   c) A homing pigeon
   d) A bucket of herring

4. **Which national team has played the most World Cup matches?**

   a) Brazil
   b) Italy
   c) England
   d) Germany (including when it was West Germany)

5. **El Salvador's 10-1 loss to Hungary in 1982 remains the biggest World Cup defeat in history. What was happening in El Salvador at that time that hindered the team's preparation and perhaps helps to explain their defeat?**

   a) A civil war, which is a type of war in which different groups in the same country fight each other
   b) Snowstorms
   c) A ban on the sale of footballs
   d) *El Salvador's Got Talent* was on TV

6. Why is Serbian midfielder Dejan Stanković unique in World Cup history?

a) He played in two World Cups, one as a goalkeeper and one as a midfielder.
b) He played in three World Cups for three different countries.
c) He played in four World Cups and scored in them all.
d) He played in five World Cups and never won a game.

7. Which team has won the World Cup a record five times?

a) England
b) Italy
c) Germany
d) Brazil

8. How was Italy striker Salvatore Schillaci remembered for finishing as the top-scorer in the 1990 World Cup?

a) He had a horse named after him.
b) He had a wine named after him.
c) He had a fashion label named after him.
d) He had a rock band named after him.

9. **Which World Cup final made history as the first to be shown live on TV?**

a) Uruguay 2 Brazil 1, 1950
b) West Germany 3 Hungary 2, 1954
c) Brazil 5 Sweden 2, 1958
d) Brazil 3 Czechoslovakia 1, 1962

10. **Which three national teams all won matches by an incredible 21–0 on their way to qualifying for the 1999 Women's World Cup?**

a) Canada, Australia, New Zealand
b) Germany, USA, Ecuador
c) China, Sweden, Nigeria
d) Belgium, Japan, Switzerland

11. Which football club has provided the most World Cup winners?

a) Juventus (Italy)
b) Bayern Munich (Germany)
c) Barcelona (Spain)
d) Santos (Brazil)

12. Why did the 1–1 draw at the 1994 World Cup match between USA and Switzerland make history?

a) Both teams had three players sent off.
b) The Swiss team sang the USA national anthem by mistake.
c) It was the first World Cup match to be played indoors.
d) The mascots of both teams started fighting with each other and had to be separated by the players.

13. **The women's football match with the highest attendance of all time was the final of the 1999 Women's World Cup, in which USA beat China. How many fans were watching in the stadium?**

   a) Around 40,000
   b) Around 90,000
   c) Around 130,000
   d) Around 200,000

14. **Who is the only footballer to have played in a World Cup final and acted in a movie that was nominated for an Oscar for the best film?**

   a) Frank Leboeuf (France), who played a doctor in *The Theory of Everything*
   b) Eric Cantona (France), who played a seagull in *Birdman*
   c) Lothar Matthäus (West Germany), who played a mathematician in *A Beautiful Mind*
   d) Pelé (Brazil), who played the king in *The King's Speech*

15. **What World Cup record does Serbian coach Bora Milutinović hold?**

   a) He is the first coach to take charge of five different teams at the World Cup.
   b) He won a World Cup in speed-eating, scoffing 37 hot dogs in ten minutes.
   c) He has been assistant coach to three World Cup winning teams.
   d) He is the only coach to be the main singer of the official World Cup anthem.

16. **The record for scoring the most goals in a single World Cup game is held by Russia's Oleg Salenko, who scored five goals in a 6–1 win during the 1994 World Cup. Who were the opponents?**

    a) England
    b) Cameroon
    c) Bolivia
    d) Greece

17. **Who is the only player to have played in three World Cup finals?**

    a) Pelé (Brazil)
    b) Cafu (Brazil)
    c) Diego Maradona (Argentina)
    d) Zinedine Zidane (France)

18. **Who was the first man to win the World Cup once as a player and then as a coach?**

    a) Mário Zagallo (Brazil)
    b) Franz Beckenbauer (Germany)
    c) Joachim Löw (Germany)
    d) Didier Deschamps (France)

19. **Wendi Henderson represented her country at two Women's World Cups played sixteen years apart: first in 1991 and then in 2007. What country was she playing for?**

a) Nigeria
b) Canada
c) USA
d) New Zealand

20. **Which player scored in the 2014 World Cup to break Ronaldo's record as the all-time leading scorer in the competition, with sixteen goals across four tournaments?**

a) Miroslav Klose (Germany)
b) Thomas Müller (Germany)
c) Arjen Robben (Netherlands)
d) Gary Lineker (England)

CANNY COACHES

Every professional football team, whether it wins or loses, has a coach. They are the ones who pick the players, choose the tactics and sometimes they get blamed, or even sacked, in case of defeat. One of the most successful coaches of all time, the Italian Giovanni Trapattoni, once said that "a good manager makes a team 10 per cent better and a bad manager makes it 30 per cent worse". We will be celebrating those brave bosses whose decisions have helped their teams at the World Cup.

The job of the coach is to improve their players and get them at their best for the big games. Some can be strict and others are friendlier. There may be lots of different ways to score in football, but the coach has one main job: to give the players the confidence to be themselves. That's the best way to get great results.

The coaches in this chapter all reached the World Cup because they knew how to get the best out of others. Now it's time to get the best out of you with these tricky coach-related questions!

1. **What is the name of the area where coaches watch the game, invented in 1931 as a sheltered area for them to take notes?**

    a) Dug-out
    b) Snug-out
    c) Bug-out
    d) Rug-out

2. **What was the name of the coach in charge of England when they won the 1966 World Cup?**

    a) Vittorio Pozzo
    b) Carlos Bilardo
    c) Alf Ramsey
    d) José Mourinho

3. **What happened to France coach Michel Hidalgo the day before the team flew to Argentina to play in the 1978 World Cup?**

    a) He got married.
    b) He escaped from a kidnap attempt.
    c) He was awarded Argentine nationality.
    d) He was sacked from his job.

4. In the 40 years between 1966 and 2006, Mário Zagallo was coach of Brazil in three World Cups and assistant coach in two World Cups. He was also very superstitious about a particular number: always wearing an item of clothing with the number on and having it on his car licence plate. What number was it?

a) 3

b) 7

c) 13

d) 666

5. How did Colombia's assistant coach Hernán Darío Gómez, who went on to coach the team in the 1998 competition, calm his nerves on the night before a game at the 1990 World Cup?

a) He did keepy-uppies in the hotel lobby all through the night.

b) He wrote a book of poetry which became a bestseller.

c) He swam 200 lengths of the hotel pool naked.

d) He slept in the same bed as coach Francisco Maturana.

6. **What did Argentina coach Daniel Passarella ban his players from doing before the 1998 World Cup?**

   a) Growing long hair
   b) Getting married
   c) Buying new football boots
   d) Playing computer games

7. **Before the 2002 World Cup, Brazil coach Luiz Felipe Scolari made a promise to do something if his team won the trophy. When his team won he stuck to his word. What did he do?**

   a) Walked ten miles on foot to a Catholic shrine
   b) Appeared on Brazilian TV in his underpants
   c) Ate 2002 bananas
   d) Sung the Brazilian national anthem dressed up as the World Cup trophy

8. **Raymond Domenech, who coached France to the 2006 World Cup final, had an unusual way of deciding which players to select. He selected players based on their star signs. For example, he did not like having Leos in defence because he thought they would show off. What is the study of star signs known as?**

   a) Horoscoplogy
   b) Zodiacology
   c) Astrology
   d) Signology

9. **As he had promised, Italy coach Marcello Lippi jumped into the lake at the team hotel after winning the 2006 World Cup final. When he emerged from the water, what was he holding?**

    a) A treasure chest
    b) The World Cup trophy
    c) Italy captain Fabio Cannavaro
    d) A large salmon

10. **Marc Wilmots played in the 1998 and 2002 World Cups for Belgium, and then coached them in 2014. But what did he spend two years doing between playing and coaching?**

    a) Climbing Mount Everest
    b) Working as a politician in the Belgian Senate
    c) Learning fluent Mandarin
    d) Dancing ballet professionally

11. **Why did Argentina coach Diego Maradona, who captained his team to World Cup success in 1986, grow a beard before the 2010 World Cup?**

   a) His dog bit his mouth and he wanted to cover the scar.

   b) Beards bring good luck in Argentina.

   c) His chin was cold.

   d) He was inspired by former US president Abraham Lincoln, who had a beard.

12. **What was World Cup-winning coach Joachim Löw caught on camera doing during Germany's 2010 World Cup semi-final against Spain?**

   a) Kissing the referee as the teams went off at half-time

   b) Picking his nose and then eating his bogey

   c) Putting three chocolate bars into his mouth at the same time

   d) Sucking his thumb

13. **What title was coach Vicente del Bosque awarded after guiding Spain to glory at the 2010 World Cup and the 2012 European Championship?**

   a) Conde Crack

   b) Vizconde Vicente

   c) Baron de Ballon D'Or

   d) First Marquis of Del Bosque

14. Because former Sweden and USA women's coach Pia Sundhage used to sing in press conferences, what did the USA players give her as a present after reaching the 2011 Women's World Cup final?

a) A microphone

b) Singing lessons

c) A guitar

d) A bouquet of flowers

15. Former West Germany striker Jürgen Klinsmann won the World Cup in 1990. Which two countries did he then manage in the tournament in 2006 and 2014?

a) Germany and USA

b) Germany and England

c) Germany and Hungary

d) Germany and Iceland

16. **Why will Ottmar Hitzfeld, the coach of Switzerland in the 2014 World Cup, never be forgotten in the Swiss village of Gspon?**

a) The Ottmar Hitzfeld Gspon Arena, the highest football pitch in Europe, is there.

b) The most popular restaurant is called Ottmar's Diner and serves chocolate footballs with every meal.

c) The main street is called Hitzfeldstrasse.

d) He represented Gspon in the Swiss Yodelling Championships for 20 years running.

17. **Complete the following sequence: Fabio Capello, Roy Hodgson, Sam Allardyce … (A clue: Three Lions!)**

a) Zinedine Zidane

b) Pep Guardiola

c) Gareth Southgate

d) Steve McClaren

18. **In 2015, the 2018 World Cup host country Russia appointed a coach, Leonid Slutsky, who had ended his playing career after a strange injury when he was 19. What happened?**

a) His mother ran him over by mistake.

b) He fell out of a tree trying to rescue a neighbour's cat.

c) A venomous snake bit him on the foot.

d) He lost an arm in a skiing accident.

19. **How did German women's coach Silvia Neid make history in 2016?**

a) She picked a team of players called Silvia to play in the 2016 Olympic final against Sweden.

b) She became the first coach to win FIFA women's coach of the year award three times.

c) She picked her daughter and granddaughter to play for the Germany national team.

d) She picked herself to play upfront when striker Anja Mittag was injured in the warm-up.

20. **The job of the coach is to get the best out of each player in every game. This might not be easy as every player is different. What is the word used to describe someone who can do this well?**

a) Motivator

b) Marketer

c) Moderator

d) Meerkat

NAUGHTY NICKNAMES

Do you follow the Three Lions? The Samurai Blues? The Super Eagles? Are you in the Tartan Army? And who's your favourite player? Kun? Hulk?

Football is full of nicknames. Clubs have nicknames, such as the Magpies (Newcastle) and the Seagulls (Brighton). As we'll see in this chapter national teams have nicknames too. Some are also birds, such as the Super Eagles (Nigeria) and the Green Falcons (Saudi Arabia). And players have nicknames, which can tell us interesting things about their background or character. Fans often like to call players by their nicknames as it makes them feel closer to them, as if they are their friends.

When it comes to clubs and national teams, a nickname is good for morale as it gives fans an affectionate way to talk about their team and helps the team have a strong sense of identity. Often the nickname of a national team relates to a symbol from the nation's history and culture, so it is a way of bringing fans together, by reminding them of what they share.

In some countries, such as Brazil, many players are known by their nicknames. One of the greatest players of all time was called Edson Arantes do Nascimento, but everyone calls him by his childhood nickname, Pelé. Now let's go around the world and play the name game!

1. **Why are the England team also known as the Three Lions and the England women's team the Lionesses?**

   a) Three lions were depicted on the first royal coat of arms of England in the reign of King Richard I in the twelfth century.
   b) Three lions escaped from London Zoo and ran onto the pitch during England's first international match at Wembley.
   c) Lions are well-known for being talented footballers.
   d) The Three Lions was the favourite pub of World Cup-winning captain Bobby Moore.

2. **The Italy national team are nicknamed the "Azzuri", or the Blues. What colours are in the Italian flag?**

   a) Blue, white and red
   b) Green, white and red
   c) Green, white and blue
   d) Navy blue, sky blue and royal blue

3. **What is the nickname of Spain's national team?**

   a) *La Furia Roja* (The Red Fury)
   b) *La Pasión Roja* (The Red Passion)
   c) *La Ira Roja* (The Red Anger)
   d) *La Nariz Roja* (The Red Nose)

4. **The Norwegian national women's team are called the:**

   a)

   b)

   c)

   d)

5. **Algeria's nickname is the Fennec Foxes, which are small foxes that live in the Sahara desert. What is the their distinguishing characteristic?**

   a) Unusually large feet, good for walking on hot sand
   b) Unusually large ears, good for losing body heat
   c) Unusually large nose, good for poking down holes when looking for food
   d) Unusually large tail, good for brushing sand off their fur

6. The African country Ivory Coast gained its name because when European explorers landed there in the fifteenth and sixteenth centuries, the main trade was ivory from elephant tusks. This is also why the Africa national team are called the Elephants. How many species of elephant are there in Africa?

a) 1
b) 2
c) 3
d) 4

7. Which African country is nicknamed the Blue Sharks?

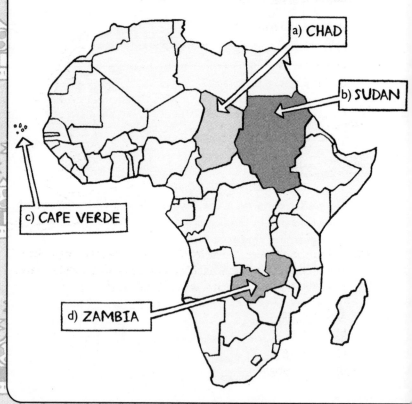

a) CHAD
b) SUDAN
c) CAPE VERDE
d) ZAMBIA

8. **Why is Iran's nickname Team Melli?**

   a) Mohammed Melli was the first ever scorer for the Iran national team in a 1–0 win over India in 1941.
   b) Mustafa Melli was the coach when Iran reached its first World Cup in 1978, when it managed a 1–1 draw with Scotland.
   c) Melli means the best in Persian, so it means the "best team".
   d) Melli means national in Persian, so it means the "national team".

9. **Japan's national team are called the Samurai Blues. What is a samurai?**

   a) A fast and nimble fish
   b) An elite warrior from ancient Japan
   c) A striker who can't stop scoring
   d) The fastest train in Japan

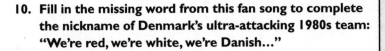

10. **Fill in the missing word from this fan song to complete the nickname of Denmark's ultra-attacking 1980s team: "We're red, we're white, we're Danish…"**

    a) Dynamite
    b) Pastries
    c) Fly-by-night
    d) If that's alright

11. **What are the Australia women's team also known as?**

    a) The Matildas
    b) The Sheilas
    c) The Socceroos
    d) The Wallabies

12. **What extinct animal, which was only ever found on the island of Mauritius in the Indian Ocean, is the nickname of the Mauritius national team?**

    a) The Dinosaurs
    b) The Dodos
    c) The Tecopa Pupfishes
    d) The Woolly Mammoths

13. **What was the nickname of Italy forward Roberto Baggio, who missed the penalty-kick that won the 1994 World Cup final for Brazil?**

    a) *Il Divin Codino* (The Divine Ponytail)
    b) *Il Bell'Uomo* (The Beautiful Man)
    c) *Il Tranquillo Perdente* (The Quiet Loser)
    d) *Calcio di Rigore Salsiccia* (The Penalty Sausage)

14. What animal is *La Pulga*, the nickname by which Argentina forward Lionel Messi is known?

a) Hornet

b) Flea

c) Cockroach

d) Termite

15. What did teammates call Spanish defender César Azpilicueta after he joined Chelsea in 2012, one year before he represented Spain in the 2014 World Cup?

a) Emperor

b) Azpi

c) Leftie

d) Dave

16. **Former Russia goalkeeper Lev Yashin played in four World Cups and is the only goalkeeper to have won the Ballon D'Or for best player in the world. Why was he called the Black Spider?**

   a) He collected spiders at his home in Moscow.
   b) He always played in a black shirt, black shorts and black gloves.
   c) He had eight legs which helped him make more saves.
   d) Yashin is the Russian word for tarantula.

17. **Many Brazilian nicknames are made by adding the letters "inho" to the end of a first name, so Fernando becomes Fernandinho, Paulo becomes Paulinho and Ronaldo becomes Ronaldinho. What does the "inho" mean?**

   a) Little, so Fernandinho means "Little Fernando"
   b) Big, so Fernandinho means "Big Fernando"
   c) Brilliant, so Fernandinho means "Brilliant Fernando"
   d) Rubbish, so Fernandinho means "Rubbish Fernando"

18. **The Brazilian known by the nickname Dunga was captain when Brazil won the 1994 World Cup. Dunga is the Portuguese translation of which dwarf from the Snow White fairytale?**

   a) Dopey
   b) Sleepy
   c) Grumpy
   d) Skilful

19. **South Korea men's team are known as the Taegeuk Warriors and the women's team are the Taegeuk Ladies. The Taegeuk symbolizes harmony and unity and appears in the middle of the South Korean flag. Which of these symbols is it?**

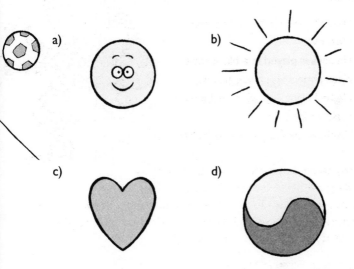

a)

b)

c)

d)

20. **When Italy hosted (and won) the World Cup in 1934, one of most famous coaches in Italy was an Englishman, William Garbutt. In an almost 40-year career there, he coached Genoa, Roma, Napoli and AC Milan. The respect that he commanded from his players is the reason that Italian footballers, to this day, refer to their coach by an English word. What is it?**

a) M'lud
b) Boss
c) Sir
d) Mister

NUMBERS GAME

Football fans are always counting down the days before the World Cup begins.

And once the tournament has started, our heads are always full of numbers, such as the squad numbers of our favourite players, kick-off times, score-lines, temperatures, goal tallies, ages of players, match schedules and distances travelled between games.

For this chapter we have found some of our favourite World Cup numbers. Alex has also sneaked in some simple maths questions to keep you on your toes. You don't need to be a maths genius to solve them, you only need to be a football fan! Can we count you in? Five, four, three, two, one...

SQUAD NUMBERS
GOAL TALLIES
TOP SCORERS
MATCH SCHEDULES
PAIRS OF CLEAN SOCKS

1. **Here are 11 famous World Cup winners. Can you guess their squad numbers from 1 to 11, with no number appearing more than once? One is a trick – can you spot it?**

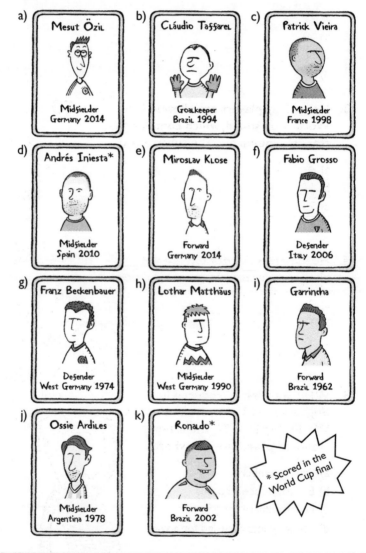

a) Mesut Özil — Midfielder, Germany 2014

b) Cláudio Taffarel — Goalkeeper, Brazil 1994

c) Patrick Vieira — Midfielder, France 1998

d) Andrés Iniesta* — Midfielder, Spain 2010

e) Miroslav Klose — Forward, Germany 2014

f) Fabio Grosso — Defender, Italy 2006

g) Franz Beckenbauer — Defender, West Germany 1974

h) Lothar Matthäus — Midfielder, West Germany 1990

i) Garrincha — Forward, Brazil 1962

j) Ossie Ardiles — Midfielder, Argentina 1978

k) Ronaldo* — Forward, Brazil 2002

* Scored in the World Cup final

2. **If the eleven players in a starting line-up have the squad numbers from I to 11, what is the sum of the numbers of the members of that team who are on the pitch at kick-off?**

   a) 12
   b) 50
   c) 66
   d) 100

3. **How many players are allowed in a World Cup squad, which contains the starting line-up and the substitutes?**

   a) 4
   b) 17
   c) 20
   d) 23

4. **How many substitutions are you allowed to make per game?**

   a) 2
   b) 3
   c) 4
   d) 5

5. **What was first introduced in England in 1981, introduced to the World Cup in 1994, and is now standard practice everywhere?**

   a) Squad numbers
   b) Electronic scoreboards
   c) Fourth official
   d) Three points awarded for a win

6. How many countries are members of FIFA, which means they are allowed to take part in qualification rounds for the World Cup?

a) 111
b) 161
c) 211
d) 261

7. If there are six teams in a World Cup qualifying group, and every team plays each other home and away, how many games are there in that group in total?

a) 12
b) 18
c) 24
d) 30

8. The 2002 World Cup final between Brazil and Germany took place in Yokohama, Japan, where the kick-off was at 8pm local time. At that moment, what time was it on the opposite side of the world, in Rio de Janeiro, Brazil?

a) 4 am
b) 8 am
c) Noon
d) 4 pm

9. **How many goals were scored during all 64 matches at the 2014 World Cup?**

   a) 71
   b) 121
   c) 171
   d) 221

10. **The 1954 World Cup had the highest number of goals per game, with 5.4 goals on average. The 1990 World Cup had the lowest, with 2.2 goals on average. What was the average number of goals per game at the 2014 World Cup? (If you got Question 9 correct, you'll be able to calculate the answer.)**

   a) 2.3
   b) 2.7
   c) 3.1
   d) 4.2

1954   BRAZIL   4.1

SWITZERLAND 1.3

We saw 5.4 goals in total.

I told you it was an average game!

11. How many possible score-lines are there if you know that three goals have been scored in a game?

a) 1
b) 2
c) 3
d) 4

12. In football the word "nil" is used for "zero" when describing the number of goals a team has scored. What word is used for zero in tennis?

a) Diddlysquat
b) Out
c) Nothing
d) Love

13. In the 1982 World Cup, Norman Whiteside of Northern Ireland became the youngest player to play in a World Cup. He was 17 years and 41 days. In 1999, Ifeanyichukwu Chiejine of Nigeria became the youngest player to play in a Women's World Cup. How old was she?

   a) 14 years, 34 days
   b) 15 years, 34 days
   c) 16 years, 34 days
   d) 17 years, 34 days

14. In 2014 the Colombia keeper Faryd Mondragón became the oldest player to ever play in a World Cup match. How old was he?

   a) 43
   b) 47
   c) 50
   d) 65

15. How many teams now compete in the Women's World Cup?

   a) 12
   b) 16
   c) 24
   d) 32

16. Can you count to three in the languages of these World Cup winning teams?

a) Portuguese (Brazil)
b) Spanish (Argentina, Spain, Uruguay)
c) French (France)
d) Italian (Italy)
e) German (Germany)

1) Un, deux, trois!

3) Uno, dos, tres!

2) Eins, zwei, drei!

5) Uno, due, tre!

4) Um, dois, três!

17. How many official 2018 World Cup balls does FIFA give each team to practise with – half of which are given after the tournament draw and the other half on arrival in Russia?

a) 2
b) 10
c) 60
d) As many as they like

18. **Russia, host of the 2018 World Cup, is the largest country by area in the world. What is the distance between the most westerly host city, Kaliningrad, and the most easterly host city, Yekaterinburg?**

    a) 100 miles
    b) 500 miles
    c) 1,500 miles
    d) 5,000 miles

19. **The average temperature in Yekaterinburg in June, during the World Cup, is 17°C. What is the average temperature there in January?**

    a) -5°C
    b) -13°C
    c) -20°C
    d) -30°C

20. **Between 1954 and 1978, there were 16 teams in the World Cup. Between 1982 and 1994, the number of teams was 24. Since 1998, that number has risen to 32. How many teams has FIFA decided will take part in the 2026 World Cup?**

    a) 24
    b) 32
    c) 48
    d) 96

SUPER STADIUMS

The world's most famous stadiums are landmarks: huge structures that are marvels of architecture and engineering. The expertise of so many people goes into making them look incredible – while also remaining safe for the thousands of people inside them. Stadiums bring communities together, to support the same team and cheer them on to victory (or defeat).

As you might expect, the World Cup features only the very best stadiums in each host nation. Once FIFA has decided which country will host the tournament, the organizers ensure each stadium meets certain strict conditions to qualify for putting on games. These include details about safe access to the stadium, supporter comfort, width of the players' tunnel and even the ideal

direction of the pitch (the preferred option is north-to-south, though it depends on where the sun might be). FIFA also requests a minimum capacity of 60,000 people for the final – which could mean a long queue for the loo at half-time!

In recent competitions, World Cup hosts provide between ten and twelve different stadiums spread out in various cities throughout the country. The exception was in 2002, when Japan and South Korea were joint hosts: then an incredible twenty stadiums (ten from each country) were used.

Join us on our world tour to discover more about these incredible venues. Your excitement levels will be at fever pitch once you get started! But this quiz is not just about the bricks and mortar…

1. **The world's first sports stadium was built in ancient Greece in order to host which event?**

    a) The Olympic Games
    b) The Gladiator Cup
    c) The World Cup
    d) The Zeus Cup

2. **What colour was the grass when the first World Cup took place in 1930?**

    a) Black and white
    b) Green
    c) Blue
    d) Purple

3. **Which stadium has a capacity of 114,000, making it the largest in the world?**

    a) Rungrado 1st of May Stadium, Pyongyang, North Korea
    b) Maracanã Stadium, Rio de Janeiro, Brazil
    c) Wembley Stadium, London, UK
    d) Bird's Nest Stadium, Beijing, China

4. **Why is a stadium called a stadium?**

    a) It comes from the Latin word *stadium*, meaning home to many.
    b) It comes from the Lithuanian word *stadio*, meaning place of joy.
    c) It comes from the ancient Greek word *stadion*, meaning a distance of about 200m.
    d) It come from the Icelandic word *staadem*, meaning "I'm cold, would you like a cup of tea?".

5. **Match these nine World Cup final stadiums to their European cities?**

a) Olympiastadion
b) Olympiastadion
c) Råsunda Stadium
d) Santiago Bernabéu
e) Stade de France
f) Stadio Olimpico
g) Wembley Stadium
h) Wankdorf Stadium
i) Luzhniki Stadium

1) Bern
2) Berlin
3) Madrid
4) Paris
5) London
6) Rome
7) Moscow
8) Stockholm
9) Munich

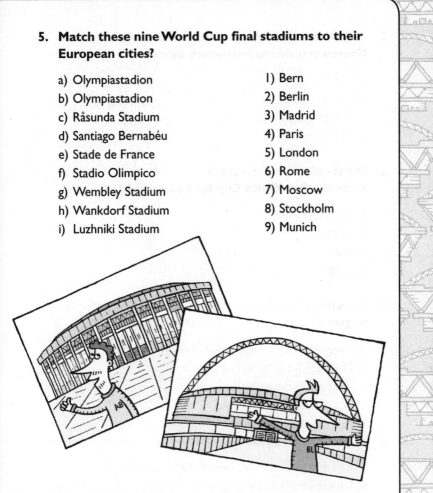

6. **Which national team has played in more than 70 stadiums in its own country, making it the team that has played in the highest number of home stadiums?**

a) Spain
b) England
c) China
d) USA

7. **Playing at high altitude – where the pitch is higher above sea level than usual – is difficult. The air is thinner, so there is less oxygen and players find it harder to breathe. Which of these stadiums is at 2,200m above sea level, making it the stadium at the highest altitude to have hosted a World Cup final?**

a) Estadio Azteca, Mexico City
b) Soccer City, Johannesburg, South Africa
c) Rose Bowl, California, USA
d) Estadio Nacional, Santiago, Chile

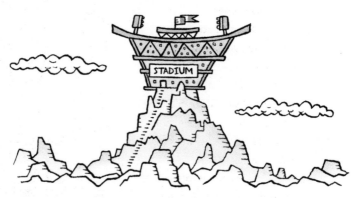

8. **Why was the 1966 World Cup group game between France and Uruguay moved from Wembley Stadium to White City Stadium?**

a) It clashed with the regular Friday afternoon greyhound racing at Wembley.
b) The groundsman needed more time to prepare the pitch for England's game against Mexico the next day.
c) Wembley's toilets got blocked during the previous game and the stadium stank.
d) Newspapers printed reports that a wizard had cast a spell on the pitch, which many fans took seriously.

9. The phrase "white elephant" means an expensive but useless possession. It is often used to describe the expensive stadiums built to host the World Cup that are hardly ever used once the tournament ends. How did the phrase come about?

a) White Elephant was a brand of luxury limousines that were too expensive to run.

b) White elephants were the most expensive flowers in Edwardian times.

c) Ancient kings in Southeast Asia would give white elephants as gifts to courtiers that annoyed them, because although a sign of honour, the elephants were difficult and expensive to look after.

d) White elephants used to be fashionable pets for the richest Victorian footballers.

10. What invention did engineer John Alexander Brodie introduce to improve football in 1891, which by the time the World Cup started in 1930 was used in all matches?

a) Special grass paint for marking out the pitch

b) Goal nets to keep fans off the pitch and prove the ball went between the two posts

c) A tunnel from the changing rooms to the pitch

d) Seats for the coaches on the touchline

11. **What is the inspiration behind the shape of the Al-Shamal Stadium in Qatar planned for the 2022 World Cup?**

a) A palm tree
b) A fishing boat
c) A football
d) An Arab tent

12. **The Maracanã Stadium in Brazil hosted the 1950 and 2014 World Cup finals. The word _maracanã_ comes from the language of the indigenous people who used to live in that area. What does it mean?**

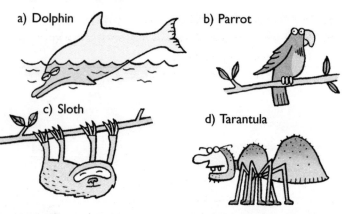

a) Dolphin

b) Parrot

c) Sloth

d) Tarantula

13. **Archibald Leitch was a famous designer of English stadiums in the first half of the twentieth century. Six of the eight stadiums used in the 1966 World Cup in England were designed, at least in part, by him. Where was Archibald from?**

a) Brazil
b) Spain
c) Liechtenstein
d) Scotland

14. **To get into a stadium you pass through a turnstile, a gate with a turning mechanism that means people can only pass through one by one. What is a "stile", which is the origin of the word "turnstile"?**

a) A stylish farmer

b) A windmill

c) A structure at the edge of a field or pen that means humans can get out but animals can't

d) A trap door

15. **Why did the players complain about the pitches at the 2015 Women's World Cup hosted in Canada?**

a) They developed a special type of blue grass.

b) They were made out of artificial turf and not real grass.

c) They smelled of maple syrup.

d) They used moose poo as a fertilizer.

16. **Which two host stadiums from the same World Cup are the furthest distance apart?**

a) Rose Bowl, Pasadena, and Foxboro Stadium, Boston, USA 1994

b) Jeju World Cup Stadium, Seogwipo, South Korea, and Sapporo Dome, Sapporo, Japan 2002

c) Estádio Castelão, Fortaleza, and Estádio Beira-Rio, Porto-Alegre, Brazil 2014

d) Saint Petersburg Stadium, Krestovsky Island, and Fisht Olympic Stadium, Sochi, Russia 2018

17. **In which landscape are each of the following World Cup host cities situated?**

a) Manaus, Brazil

b) Polokwane, South Africa

c) Orlando, USA

d) Sandviken, Sweden

1) Pine forest

2) Swamp

3) Savannah

4) Rainforest

18. **The Estadio Carlos Dittborn in the Chilean city of Arica was one of the four host cities in the 1962 World Cup. What is famous about Arica?**

   a) The windiest inhabited place in the world.
   b) The driest inhabited place in the world.
   c) The hottest inhabited place in the world.
   d) The chilliest inhabited place in the world.

19. **Wembley Stadium got its name from the London suburb of Wembley where it is located. But how did Wembley get its name?**

   a) It used to be an area of forest inhabited by mythical creatures called Wembles.
   b) It used to be a clearing owned by the Wemba family.
   c) Its first inhabitant was William Wembley, who set up London's first football boot-maker there.
   d) It is a mispronunciation of "wobbly", which was used in medieval times to describe the bumpy track through the area, one of the main roads out of London.

20. **The Estadio Azteca in Mexico was the first stadium to host two World Cup finals in 1970 and 1986. Who or what are Aztecs?**

   a) A group of nineteenth century Mexican revolutionaries
   b) The people who lived in Mexico before it was invaded by European explorers in the sixteenth century
   c) Members of the very first Mexican football team
   d) A type of eagle only found in Mexico

HEROES AND VILLAINS

Heroes are the people whose achievements and courage stand above all others, and whose behaviour is often responsible for great victories. Villains, on the other hand, sometimes act out of malice and their behaviour is often responsible for failures. Football may be a team sport but the World Cup produces lots of heroes and villains. We will meet some of them here.

The pressure on players at a World Cup is enormous: whole countries are cheering them on in support, and just as one goal can change the course of a player's career, so can one mistake. Almost every match has its own hero and villain, especially as many goals come as the result of a mistake somewhere along the way!

HEROES

In some cases, players can be a hero and a villain in the same game, like Dutch defender Ernie Brandts. He played in the 1978 World Cup fixture against Italy and put the ball past his own goalkeeper in the first half to give the Italians a lead. In the second half, he equalized and the Netherlands won the game 2–1. Brandts was the first player to score for both teams in the same World Cup game. A villain! And a hero! Well done, Ernie!

In this chapter, let's start with the good guys before getting to the baddies…

VILLAINS

1. **Uruguay forward Alcides Ghiggia was the hero of the 1950 World Cup final, scoring the winning goal against hosts Brazil. But he then moved country and ended up playing for his new national team. Which country was it?**

   a) Brazil
   b) Argentina
   c) Spain
   d) Italy

2. **What kit-related problem made French goal-scoring hero Just Fontaine's tally of thirteen goals in the 1958 World Cup especially impressive?**

   a) His shorts kept on falling down, so he had to attach them to his shirt with safety pins.
   b) He was wearing a pair of boots borrowed from a teammate.
   c) He wore two pair of socks on each foot as he had particularly cold ankles.
   d) He had to wear silk pants and a silk vest since his skin had an allergic reaction to cotton.

3. **Why was Geoff Hurst, who scored a hat-trick in the 1966 World Cup final for England, an unlikely hero in the team?**

   a) He was only playing because first-choice striker Jimmy Greaves was injured.
   b) He was a goalkeeper who had never played as a striker before.
   c) He was born in West Germany, who were England's final opponents.
   d) He was playing in slippers as he'd left his boots at home.

4. **What did the dog Pickles do that turned him into a hero of the 1966 World Cup?**

   a) He barked a hilarious rendition of *God Save the Queen* during the World Cup final half-time entertainment.
   b) He ran onto the pitch during the England v. West Germany final and distracted the German goalkeeper by doing a poo by the posts.
   c) He found the World Cup trophy in a London garden, which had been stolen a few days before.
   d) He was Wembley's guard dog and fought off burglars trying to steal the World Cup balls the night before the final.

5. **Eusébio, the forward who scored a heroic nine goals for Portugal in the 1966 World Cup, was born in which African country that was at that time a Portuguese colony?**

   a) Cape Verde
   b) Mozambique
   c) São Tomé and Principe
   d) Angola

6. **Dutch winger Johan Cruyff's famous "Cruyff turn" was a move in which he faced one way, side-heeled the ball away from him and span and sprinted off with the ball, leaving his marker confused and dizzy. His first did it against Swedish defender Jan Olsson at the 1974 World Cup. How did Olsson describe this moment later?**

a) "The worst moment of my career."
b) "The proudest moment of my career."
c) "The funniest moment of my career."
d) "The strangest moment of my career."

7. **Brazil's 1982 World Cup captain Sócrates was named after an ancient Greek what?**

a) Sailor
b) Shopkeeper
c) Footballer
d) Philosopher

8. **Roger Milla was a hero for Cameroon in the 1990 World Cup, scoring four goals and helping the Indomitable Lions become the first African side to reach the quarter final. How did he celebrate his goals?**

a) He ran to the corner flag and wiggled his hips.
b) He kissed the referee.
c) He walked on his hands.
d) He imitated a lion, opening his mouth like he was roaring and holding his hands up as if to show off his claws.

9. **USA midfielder Carli Lloyd is a national hero for her amazing performances: she scored the winning goal in the 2008 and 2012 Olympic finals, and she netted a hat-trick in the 2015 Women's World Cup final. How did she describe her unique twice-daily training routine, which did not even stop for Christmas Day?**

a) "Why would I want to be like everyone else?"
b) "You have to work hard to score goals!"
c) "Goals taste better than mince pies!"
d) "Running is my fuel!"

10. **Argentina captain Antonio Rattín was the villain in a bad-tempered 1966 World Cup quarter-final against England, in which he was sent off in the first half for arguing with the referee. When he finally left the pitch, he infuriated the England fans at Wembley by doing what?**

a) He flashed his bottom to the crowd as he walked off.
b) He wiped his hands on an England flag as he left the pitch.
c) He sat on the touchline and refused to move when asked.
d) He went to the Wembley electricity-box and turned off the floodlights.

11. **West Germany goalkeeper Harald Schumacher became the villain of the 1982 World Cup when he seriously injured France forward Patrick Battiston. In the days after, who had to intervene to ensure relations between the two countries remained friendly?**

   a) The players' mothers
   b) West German chancellor Helmut Schmidt and French president François Mitterrand
   c) The referee Charles Corver
   d) The FIFA president at the time João Havelange

12. **Defender Rigobert Song became the first World Cup player to be sent off in two different tournaments, in 1994 and 1998. Which country did he play for?**

   a) France
   b) Colombia
   c) Mexico
   d) Cameroon

13. **Being sent off does not guarantee that your team will lose the game. One player was sent off in a World Cup final, but then later celebrated as a hero after his team went on to lift the trophy. Who was it?**

   a) Gustavo Dezotti (Argentina 1990)
   b) Marcel Desailly (France 1998)
   c) Zinedine Zidane (France 2006)
   d) John Heitinga (Netherlands 2010)

14. **How did Ireland captain and bad boy Roy Keane make headlines the day before his team's first match in the 2002 World Cup in Japan?**

   a) His dog bit the team chef after he gave it over-cooked steak.
   b) He quit the squad complaining that the team's preparations were amateur.
   c) He got a tattoo which read, "I hate football".
   d) He applied for Japanese citizenship.

15. **Portugal forward Cristiano Ronaldo was his country's hero when they beat England in the 2006 World Cup quarter-final. But he was seen as a villain by England fans because he made what cheeky celebration when Wayne Rooney got sent off?**

   a) He winked
   b) He gave the thumbs up
   c) He laughed out loud
   d) He pretended to play the violin

16. **Why was France striker Nicolas Anelka sent home during the 2010 World Cup?**

   a) He swore at the coach during a half-time argument.
   b) He would not stop farting on the team coach.
   c) His jokes were the worst in the team.
   d) He snored so loudly it kept the whole team awake.

17. How did the Netherlands midfielder Nigel de Jong make his presence felt in the first half of the 2010 World Cup final against Spain?

a) He scored an own goal.

b) He tripped up Spain coach Vicente del Bosque when chasing a ball.

c) He kicked opponent Xabi Alonso in the chest.

d) He threw the referee's whistle into the crowd.

18. Uruguay forward Luis Suárez was the villain of the 2014 World Cup after he bit the shoulder of Italy defender Giorgio Chiellini. What was FIFA's punishment?

a) They banned him from watching the World Cup for the next six weeks.

b) They banned him from playing football for four months and he had to miss nine Uruguay games.

c) They banned him from biting any food and he was only allowed to drink smoothies for three months.

d) They sent him straight to bed without dinner. All was fine the next day when he had said sorry.

19. **Why did Argentina's fans blame forward Gonzalo Higuaín for losing the 2014 World Cup final to Germany?**

    a) He missed the best chance of the game before Germany scored.

    b) He played with his socks rolled down, which is bad luck in Argentina.

    c) He had a cold and infected the other players with it.

    d) He was waving to his mum in the crowd when Germany scored.

20. **Lionel Messi was a hero helping Argentina reach one World Cup final and three Copa America finals (the competition for South America's best national team), even though his team lost all four. Why did fans criticise him during the 2018 World Cup qualifying matches?**

    a) He missed every penalty he took.

    b) He grew a beard.

    c) He didn't sing the national anthem before games.

    d) He picked the team.

QUIZ ANSWERS

WONDERFUL WORLD

1. d
2. a
3. d
4. b
5. a
6. 1) USA, 2) Mexico, 3) Brazil,
   4) Chile, 5) Argentina,
   6) Uruguay, 7) Sweden,
   8) England, 9) Germany,
   10) France, 11) Switzerland,
   12) Spain, 13) Italy, 14) Russia,
   15) South Korea, 16) Japan,
   17) Qatar, 18) South Africa
7. d
8. b
9. d
10. b
11. c
12. d
13. b
14. d
15. b
16. a
17. d
18. b
19. d
20. a) 3, b) 4, c) 1, d) 2, e) 6, f) 5

GREAT GOALS

1. c
2. c
3. a
4. a
5. d
6. a
7. c
8. c
9. a
10. b
11. b
12. a
13. c
14. a
15. b
16. c
17. b
18. b
19. c
20. b

REFS AND RED CARDS	OUCHY INJURIES
1. c	1. a
2. a	2. b
3. c	3. b
4. a	4. b
5. b	5. a
6 d	6. c
7. a	7. b
8. c	8. 1) Clavicle, 2) Femur,
9. b	3) Patella, 4)Tibia,
10. b	5) Fibula, 6) Metatarsal
11. d	9. b
12. c	10. a
13. b	11. c
14. b	12. a
15. a	13. b
16. b	14. c
17. a	15. d
18. c	16. a
19. b	17. b
20. c	18. d
	19. b
	20. a

QUIZ ANSWERS

QUIZ

ANSWERS

PRESSURE PENALTIES

1. c
2. a
3. d
4. b
5. b
6. b
7. a
8. d
9. c
10. b
11. a
12. c
13. c
14. b
15. a
16. a
17. c
18. d
19. c
20. b

SHOCK RESULTS

1. a
2. b
3. a
4. b, a, d
5. b
6. b
7. c
8. b
9. d
10. b
11. d
12. a
13. b
14. c
15. a
16. b
17. a
18. b
19. d
20. a) 1, b) 3, c) 2,
    d) 4, e) 6, f) 5

MIGHTY MASCOTS	JEEPERS KEEPERS
1. a	1. d
2. a	2. c
3. a	3. c
4. b	4. a
5. a	5. b
6 c	6. b
7. b	7. a
8. c	8. b
9. d	9. c
10. a	10. a
11. b	11. a
12. c	12. d
13. b	13. a
14. d	14. a
15. b	15. b
16. c	16. b
17. a	17. a
18. d	18. b
19. a	19. b
20. d	20. a

HAPPY FAMILIES

1. c
2. a
3. a
4. c
5. a
6. a
7. b
8. a
9. c
10. a
11. d
12. c
13. a
14. a
15. a
16. d
17. b
18. b
19. c
20. b

RECORD BREAKERS

1. c
2. c
3. b
4. d
5. a
6. b (Yugoslavia, Serbia & Montenegro, Serbia)
7. d
8. a
9. b
10. a
11. a (prior to the 2018 Word Cup)
12. c
13. b
14. a
15. a (Mexico, Costa Rica, USA, Nigeria, China)
16. b
17. b
18. a
19. d
20. a

CANNY COACHES	NAUGHTY NICKNAMES
1. a	1. a
2. c	2. b
3. b	3. a
4. c	4. c
5. d	5. b
6 a	6. b
7. a	7. c
8. c	8. d
9. d	9. b
10. b	10. a
11. a	11. a
12. b	12. b
13. d	13. a
14. c	14. b
15. a	15. d
16. a	16. b
17. c	17. a
18. b	18. a
19. b	19. d
20. a	20. d

NUMBERS GAME

1. a) 8, b) 1, c) 4, d) 6, e) 11, f) 3, g) 5, h) 10, i) 7, j) 2, k) 9
   Trick: Ossie Ardiles was a midfielder who wore the No 2 shirt, as Argentina ordered their numbers by alphabet not position
2. c
3. d
4. b
5. d
6. c
7. d
8. b
9. c
10. b
11. d
12. d
13. c
14. a
15. c
16. a) 4, b) 3, c) 1, d) 5, e) 2
17. c
18. c
19. b
20. c

SUPER STADIUMS

1. a
2. b
3. a
4. c
5. a) 2, b) 9, c) 8, d) 3, e) 4, f) 6, g) 5, h) 1, i) 7
6. d
7. a
8. a
9. c
10. b
11. b
12. b
13. d
14. c
15. b
16. a
17. a) 4, b) 3, c) 2, d) 1
18. b
19. b
20. b

HEROES AND VILLAINS

1. d
2. b
3. a
4. c
5. b
6. b
7. d
8. a
9. a
10. b
11. b
12. d
13. b
14. b
15. a
16. a
17. c
18. b
19. a
20. c

ACKNOWLEDGEMENTS

Final question: which football quiz book has the best team behind it? This one! Thanks to Spike Gerrell for his wonderful drawings, and everyone at Walker Books, especially Daisy Jellicoe, Denise Johnstone-Burt, Louise Jackson, Laurelie Bazin, Rosi Crawley, Alex Spears, Kirsten Cozens, Krystle Appiah and Megan Middleton. We are grateful to our agents at Janklow & Nesbit and David Luxton Associates. Extra thanks to research supremo Nick Ames, and to Philippe Auclair, Marcus Christenson, Federico Farcomeni, Stoyan Georgiev, Daniel Jammers, Scott Murray, Jen O'Neill, Lars Sivertsen, Jonathan Wilson, and Carl Worswick.

High fives to our Star Pupils, Oliver Atlay, George Galgey, Sonny Lampitt, Margot and Thibault Lyttleton, James Morgan Jnr and Harry Webb.

ABOUT YOUR COACHES

Alex Bellos writes for the *Guardian* and has written several bestselling popular science books.

Ben Lyttleton is an author, broadcaster and consultant to professional football clubs.

Spike Gerrell draws cartoons for magazines and books.

MORE FROM FOOTBALL SCHOOL

Coming soon